THE *Ten* COMMANDMENTS FOR TODAY

THE *Ten* COMMANDMENTS FOR TODAY

Edited by

JOHN G. SCOTT

Bookcraft
Salt Lake City, Utah

Library of Congress Catalog Card Number: 97–76878

ISBN 1–57008–353–3

First Printing, 1997

Printed in the United States of America

This book is dedicated to
the memory of
Eric D. Allred and Taylor R. Brady,
two young men who exemplified
the living of the Ten Commandments;
and to Rebecca, Daniel, David,
Sarah, Elizabeth, and Michael,
who are trying their best to
live the Ten Commandments
in a modern world.

Contents

Acknowledgments

I acknowledge the dedication, the excellent scholarship, and the gospel learning of authors of this book. The Bookcraft staff were most helpful, especially Cory Maxwell, who recognized the worth of this project and encouraged me to pursue it to this final conclusion. I also acknowledge the encouragement that John K. Challis, Richard D. Draper, and Valene J. Scott gave me throughout the project.

The various religious educators who wrote this book recognize the powerful message in the Ten Commandments. They love the scriptures and are dedicated to Jesus Christ and His gospel.

The views presented in this book are the responsibility of the individual authors. While the authors believe that what they have written is doctrinally true, they acknowledge that the only sure source of official pronouncement on doctrines of the Church is the First Presidency.

John G. Scott
Editor

Institutes of Biblical Law

RICHARD D. DRAPER

*T*HINKING OF HER QUESTION still amuses me. Actually it was not her question so much as the other students' reaction to it that I find humorous. She was a bright young lady and a good thinker. A mature senior in an early morning seminary class composed of students from the ninth through the twelfth grades, she had proven to be a spiritual and stabilizing influence. That's one reason why her question startled me.

We were studying the New Testament that year and had now come to the Sermon on the Mount. We were analyzing the Savior's statement, "Think not that I am come to destroy the law, or the prophets: I am not come to destroy, but to fulfil" (Matthew 5:17). I was in the process of pointing out that most of the laws

---

Richard D. Draper is an assistant professor of Ancient Scripture at Brigham Young University. He is the author of Opening the Seven Seals *and has published numerous articles in the* Ensign. *He and his wife, Barbara, live in Lindon, Utah.*

and commandments of that era, the performances and ordinances associated with the Mosaic law, are no longer to be practiced, because they were fulfilled in Christ. That's when she asked the question: "If the Ten Commandments were part of the Mosaic law, and Jesus fulfilled the law, why do we have to obey them?" "Yeah!" other students chimed in.

Either the Lord fulfilled the law or He didn't, the girl insisted, and if, as I was maintaining, He had fulfilled the law, then obedience to these commandments was no longer necessary. As the implication caught hold, some of the sharper students ventured that, since the Atonement paid for all sin, obedience to any law seemed unnecessary. There was general enthusiasm on the subject, and I still find this little trip into antinomianism quite amusing. But I could see that a few students seriously wondered how Jesus could fulfill the law, atone for sin, and still demand obedience to the Ten Commandments.

What my students had not understood was that the Ten Commandments were among the body of "great governing principles" that were revealed from heaven for the benefit of mankind in all gospel dispensations, beginning with Adam. God will never "repeal" these principles. Hence their summarizations on the Mount Sinai tablets were not part of the laws that were fulfilled with the death and resurrection of the Savior.[1]

In any case, as I explained to my class, the Savior did not fulfill the Mosaic law so that we could freely abide in sin. He fulfilled one law in order to open the way to a higher one. He moved us from the law of Moses to the law of the gospel. What we must understand is that the Ten Commandments are a part of both. The Savior sublimated them into His higher order. In the Sermon on the Mount He revealed just how He did this. For example, under His law killing is ruled out because the Saint controls his or her emotions and abides in love. Adultery is out of the question, for the Saint bridles his or her passions and never gives in to lust. (See Matthew 5:21–32.)

With that as background, my class and I went on to explore in detail the beauty and power of the law of the gospel with its associated Ten Commandments. It proved to be a memorable and worthwhile class period.

I tell this story to emphasize the point that the higher law revealed by the Savior did not do away with the Ten Commandments. Because of their association with the law of Moses, many people view them as inferior statutes, lesser laws designed for the spiritually weak. Is that true? The Lord did indeed give Israel a lesser law which, as Paul says, "was added because of transgressions, till the seed should come to whom the promise was made" (Galatians 3:19). But we should also keep in mind that the first set of tables, those made by the hand of the Lord, contained the fulness of the gospel covenant. It was the second set, which Moses made, that contained the lesser law. Consider the words of the Joseph Smith Translation:

> And the Lord said unto Moses, Hew thee two other tables of stone, like unto the first, and I will write upon them also, the words of the law, according as they were written at the first on the tables which thou brakest; but it shall not be according to the first, for I will take away the priesthood out of their midst; therefore my holy order, and the ordinances thereof, shall not go before them; for my presence shall not go up in their midst, lest I destroy them.
>
> But I will give unto them the law as at the first, but it shall be after the law of the carnal commandment; for I have sworn in my wrath, that they shall not enter into my presence, into my rest, in the days of their pilgrimage. Therefore do as I have commanded thee, and be ready in the morning, and come up in the morning unto mount Sinai, and present thyself there to me, in the top of the mount. (JST Exodus 34:1–2.)

Some items were the same on both tables. Among them were the Ten Commandments, referred to as the "the words of the covenant" (Exodus 34:27). Therefore, they were a part of both the higher and the lesser law and part of the foundation on which both were built.

How important are the Ten Commandments to the law of the gospel? The answer is, more so than most people suspect. As an introduction to the subject, consider for a moment how one's personal world would change if everyone on the earth lived the Ten Commandments. Certain occupations would lose most of their practitioners. For instance, locksmiths would find there would be a drastic drop in sales, for locks would be used mostly for privacy and to keep children safe from harmful items; they would otherwise be of little use. Police forces would be much smaller, for policemen would primarily be used for emergency purposes and public safety. A coast guard would be necessary, but what about an army, navy, or air force? And what of the law profession and the state welfare bureaucracy? Both of these would experience a marked decline in the need for their services. The list would be lengthy.

As one really takes the question seriously, it becomes apparent that our world would be vastly different. In fact, if everyone fully lived the Ten Commandments the world would no longer be at the telestial level; it would be terrestrial. To say it more strongly, these rules form the foundation for a millennial society.

Indeed, we might say that one's reach for celestial glory and perfection presumably begin with the Decalogue, as the Ten Commandments are often called. Paul, speaking of the whole law, but not excluding the Decalogue, said that "the law was our schoolmaster to bring us unto Christ, that we might be justified by faith. But after that faith is come, we are no longer under a schoolmaster" (Galatians 3:24–25). The millennial world is not the celestial world. Rather, it is preparation for it. The Ten Commandments will play their part in the millennial era, our schoolmaster preparing us to live the full law of the Lord. God has said, speaking of Zion, the eternal society, "Zion cannot be built up unless it is by the principles of the law of the celestial kingdom; otherwise I cannot receive her unto myself" (D&C 105:5). Now, Zion will exist during and will even fuel the millennial era, but we can live the full celestial law only through a rigorous course of training. That is the job of the terrestrial era. It appears that that era, along with the Ten Commandments, is the schoolmaster to bring us to God.

However, do not think of the word *schoolmaster,* as used by Paul, in terms of a modern schoolteacher. Paul used the word *paidagogos* instead of *didaskalos.*[2] The latter term denotes a teacher in the formal sense: the former describes a well-educated slave who was in charge of teaching children from Roman upper-crust homes self-control, discipline, and manners. A good English translation would be "nanny," one whose job it is to "mold the breed."[3] The nanny is not concerned with reading, writing, and arithmetic. She is concerned with proper manners, etiquette, and polite behavior. So it is with the Ten Commandments—God designed them to teach us proper devotional and societal behavior. True, in and of themselves they are insufficient for exaltation. We must live them as they are encompassed in the law of the gospel.[4] But as we live them within its context they prepare us to live God's higher order.

The law, then, and obedience to the law, is not an end in itself. God gave the law for a purpose. The Ten Commandments give us a micro-study of God's purpose in giving laws in general. This chapter explores the institutes of biblical law. The word *institute* comes from the Latin words *in* prefixed to *stituere,* which means to set up, organize, or establish.[5] This chapter looks at the basis on which God founded and organized biblical law, and more specifically the Decalogue, with emphasis on the importance, goal, and value of the law.

Just before Israel was about to go into the promised land, Moses explained God's purpose in giving them His law:

> Behold, I have taught you statutes and judgments, even as the Lord my God commanded me, that ye should do so in the land whither ye go to possess it.
>
> Keep therefore and do them; for this is your wisdom and your understanding in the sight of the nations, which shall hear all these statutes, and say, Surely this great nation is a wise and understanding people.

> For what nation is there so great, who hath God so nigh unto them, as the Lord our God is in all things that we call upon him for?
>
> And what nation is there so great, that hath statutes and judgments so righteous as all this law, which I set before you this day? (Deuteronomy 4:5–8.)

As Israel lived the law, two outcomes, the Lord taught, would impress other nations: first, that Israel had a close and intimate association with her God, and second, that her law promoted wisdom and understanding. Both of these would appeal to people of good conscience, causing them to gravitate toward Jehovah. Therefore God designed the law to accomplish two tasks: to allow Israel to become great among the family of nations, and to act as a missionary tool by which other people would come to know God and be drawn to Him. The tragedy of Israel's failure to live the law is that she failed not only God but also those nations she could have otherwise brought to Him.

But Israel's failure should not deter us from seeing God's law for what it was, a higher order of societal relationship designed to bring spirituality, peace, and love. Unlike the law codes derived by Israel's neighbors, Hebrew law was exclusively religious. Jehovah defined all associations and interactions in Israel as spiritual in nature. Here we see an example of what He has reiterated in modern times: "All things unto me are spiritual, and not at any time have I given unto you a law which was temporal; neither any man, nor the children of men" (D&C 29:34). The Lord will not allow His children to compartmentalize the secular from the sacred. For Israel (and the modern Church) all social interactions were to be regarded as sacred. In contrast, the contemporary kingdoms of the Hittites and Babylonians distinguished between religious and secular law. Religious matters were viewed as a public concern but were seen as a separate category from the law of the state. The Bible insists that there is no difference. Neither religious nor temporal spheres were a creation of the state, but of God. Therefore, the Bible views social obligation and religious duty as one.[6]

The Bible records the entire covenant code in Exodus 20:1 to 23:19. The Ten Commandments preface the whole and, thus, assert themselves as its foundation. But the organization of the rest is most telling. The forepart deals with cultic laws forbidding acts of idolatry and governing the construction of altars. It then moves on to laws dealing with servants, marriage, crimes worthy of the death penalty, and responsibility for public and private damages. The latter part deals with punishment for stealing, improper care of other people's property, lascivious acts, afflicting widows, usury, and so on.

What is of note is that at the center of these laws is a solemn *religious* prohibition that "He that sacrificeth unto any god, save unto the Lord only, he shall be utterly destroyed" (Exodus 22:20). Here we see God using a bracketing or ring composition to emphasize the religious framework of the law code as a whole. That composition underscores one major point: only when society understands its relationship with God can it define its relationship with others.[7]

God created His law to be flexible enough to accommodate His people in all situations in which they might find themselves. In order to meet changing conditions, the law demanded that people refrain from doing things "that ought not to be done" or "which are not done" (Genesis 20:9; 29:26; 34:7; 2 Samuel 13:12). In this we see that God forbade the Israelite to violate the rules of custom He had set down among them. Mitigating against harmful practices that might creep in, the law demanded that the people follow only the "way of good men" and "the paths of the righteous" (Proverbs 2:20).[8]

In giving His law, God reflected His deep desire to enter into a covenantal relationship with Israel, but there was no equality here. Jehovah initiated everything. The people did not dictate terms to God. He dictated His terms to them. However, He did not force the law upon them; it was based upon the consent of the governed. Moses' statements in Exodus clearly show that God gave the people an offer, and they accepted it by saying: "All that the Lord hath spoken we will do" (Exodus 19:8; 24:7, see also

Deuteronomy 27, where, after a recital of the laws, benedictions, and curses the people respond with "Amen").[9]

God stated clearly why He gave Israel the law: "For thou shalt worship no other god: for the Lord, whose name is Jealous, is a jealous God" (Exodus 34:14).[10] We often struggle with the idea of this kind of passion being associated with God, because we see jealousy as a base, primitive emotion. The Hebrew term that Moses used, *qânâ'*, was derived from the act of dyeing cloth an intense red or black. Out of this grew the metaphorical meaning denoting very strong emotion or feeling. *Qânâ'* came to describe that emotion which caused one to act to protect, recover, or regain a cherished object. This feeling can be translated into English by such words as *zeal, fervor,* and *ardent love.*

Jealousy in this instance means that God's justice and mercy do not act as impersonal and dispassionate forces. It expresses that part of His very nature that causes Him to act with zeal and ardent love toward His children, and especially those who come under His covenant. This love allows Him to protect them from their enemies when they are righteous and to curse them when they are disobedient. He uses the latter in His attempt to recover them from sin and apostasy. Solomon understood this. He advised his people to "despise not the chastening of the Lord; neither be weary of his correction: for whom the Lord loveth he correcteth; even as a father the son in whom he delighteth" (Proverbs 3:11–12). Correction, then, is a reflection of God's zeal for His children.

Therefore, far from being a base, primitive emotion, God's zeal or jealousy describes the mutually exclusive relationship that God attempts to establish between himself and His covenant people. Like a marriage that involves mutually exclusive rights to each partner, Israel's relationship with Jehovah excludes any competing dealings with other gods. Indeed, Jehovah claims Israel as His "peculiar treasure" (Exodus 19:5), "separated . . . from all [other] people" (Exodus 33:16). His point is that He will have no other people except those who come under His law and abide in His covenant.

Likewise, His people must have no other God.[11] The first commandment, as well as the Decalogue as a whole, protects the exclusive gift God offers Israel and Israel alone. That gift is himself. In demanding exclusive worship through obedience to His law, Jehovah defines both himself and Israel's responsibility to Him.[12] He is a God of order. As the Savior pointed out to Joseph Smith,

> Behold, mine house is a house of order, saith the Lord God, and not a house of confusion.
>
> Will I accept of an offering, saith the Lord, that is not made in my name?
>
> Or will I receive at your hands that which I have not appointed?
>
> And will I appoint unto you, saith the Lord, except it be by law, even as I and my Father ordained unto you, before the world was?
>
> I am the Lord thy God; and I give unto you this commandment—that no man shall come unto the Father but by me or by my word, which is my law, saith the Lord.
>
> And everything that is in the world, whether it be ordained of men, by thrones, or principalities, or powers, or things of name, whatsoever they may be, that are not by me or by my word, saith the Lord, shall be thrown down, and shall not remain after men are dead, neither in nor after the resurrection, saith the Lord your God. (D&C 132:8–13.)

As a God of order, He will make sure that law will prevail. Therefore, Israel will receive His blessings only as she obeys His word.

God's commandments, especially those given to His chosen people, express His love and His zeal. He promises both His power and His protection to those who know Him and attend to His law. But He promises more. God's personal presence is His greatest gift to Israel. Consider that for a moment. God's gift is himself. He told Israel: "I will set my tabernacle among you: and my soul shall not abhor you. And I will walk among you, and will be your God, and ye shall be my people." (Leviticus 26:11–12.)

The commandments show His people how to protect that gift. Therefore, God did not demand love and obedience as a means of securing His love and zeal, but as a demonstration, on Israel's part, that they accepted it and were willing to live in accordance with it.[13]

This clearly reveals God's view of His commandments. He has promised that His Latter-day Saints "shall also be crowned with blessings from above, yea, and with commandments not a few, and with revelations in their time—they that are faithful and diligent before me" (D&C 59:4). Seen in this light, keeping God's commandments transforms even the negative duty of exclusive recognition of Jehovah into the positive attitude of showing acceptance of Him and His divine goodness and grace.[14]

Jehovah made the Atonement to restore His people to a position of covenant-keeping from that of covenant-breaking.[15] The whole point of His sacrifice, as Paul noted, was to enable people to keep the law by freeing them "from the law of sin and death" (Romans 8:2), "that the righteousness of the law might be fulfilled in us" (Romans 8:4).[16] God assists those who come under His law. We define His assistance as grace. He has declared that His grace is sufficient for all those who humble themselves before Him, and that He will "make weak things become strong unto them" (Ether 12:27).

God designed the earth to be governed by those who willingly came under the power of His grace. That is, He gave authority only to those who accepted His laws and entered into His covenant. God assigned Adam with his wife, Eve, while yet in the garden, to "be fruitful, and multiply, and replenish (*mâlê'*) the earth, and subdue (*kâvash*) it: and have dominion over (*râdâh*) . . . every living thing that moveth upon the earth" (Genesis 1:28). The Hebrew word *mâlê'* carries the idea of making full or complete. Here, God gave to Adam and Eve the keys of procreation. *Kâvash* and *râdâh* are related words both meaning "to exert pressure upon." But what kind of pressure? The lexicon gives *râdâh* such meanings as rule over, plow, tread upon, trample, and chastise, while *kâvash* means to squeeze, hug, tread down, disregard, conquer, oppress, and subjugate.[17] Due to these widely different meanings, scholars have translated Adam's responsibility differently, depending on their own position as to the nature of man's dominion. Therefore, some translators say that God allowed Adam to violate the earth, while others argue that God demanded that Adam cherish it.[18]

What is the proper interpretation of God's command to Adam and Eve? In addition to the commission to fill up the earth with their offspring, Adam was given the position of lord and master over it. This delegated position essentially made him the caretaker for the Lord's creation. Thus, Adam was Michael, the name meaning "he who is as God." Adam bequeathed the same powers to his children. But, as the words the Bible uses show, dominion could take two forms. This seems very fitting, because God put us here as a test to see how we would use His powers and respond to the earth. This freedom allowed individuals to show to themselves and their fellows, and to God and His witnesses, just how they would behave when entrusted with the powers of procreation and of dominion. Those who violate the earth and others, who disregard and oppress nature, will find themselves forever banned from the powers of both creation and procreation. On the other hand, those who cherish the earth and subdue it with their own sweat and love, and strive to fill it up, will possess both powers forever.[19] The promise was that if Adam and his posterity took care of the earth, the earth would respond with her bounty. Obedience to God's laws assured Adam that he would subdue and rule over the earth in a proper manner, with everyone benefitting. Obedience guaranteed he would not harm but rather would cherish and better that which God had given him.

Some of his descendants, Cain in particular, sought to establish separate dominion and autonomous jurisdiction outside of God's order (Genesis 4:5–8). They did this by falling for the seduction of Satan who, as Enoch said, came "among the children of men, and tempteth them to worship him; and men have become carnal, sensual, and devilish, and are shut out from the presence of God" (Moses 6:49). As a consequence, they fell to sin and spiritual death, abused the earth and its riches, and lost God's kingdom in the process. In an attempt to reestablish His kingdom, Jehovah called Abraham and then Jacob and his sons, charging them, as he had Adam, with the responsibility of subduing the earth and exercising, once more, dominion under God. When He brought Israel out of captivity, the Lord called Moses and gave him His law as a means of doing the same thing.[20] But Jehovah first had to establish His covenant with Israel. Only by entering into the covenant and striving to keep it could they come under the Lord's grace. True, they were weak and could not live His law fully. However, by striving, they showed their acceptance of Him and allowed Him to extend His power to them. His purpose in extending grace, therefore, was not to annul the law, but to fulfill it and enable His people to more fully keep it unto eventual perfection.

In sum, through Moses, God gave Israel His covenant, and the Ten Commandments as its foundation. The intent was that by striving to live the covenant, the Israelites would open the way for God's grace to flow to them. By receiving His grace, Israel would be empowered to better keep His law. As they better kept the law, additional power would flow. Eventually, through the grace of God, they would be able to live His law perfectly. During the period of growth, Jehovah would be near His people as they established the kingdom of God on the earth. Once His kingdom was restored, other nations would be drawn to Jehovah due to His presence with His people, the enlightened nature of their laws, and the peace, prosperity, and love they possessed.

With an understanding that God designed His law to bring grace to Israel and facilitate its perfection, we are ready to explore the nature of the law. The Bible teaches us three important facts. First, the law was derived from revelation. The Hebrew word for law, *torah*, denotes instruction or authoritative direction.[21] The word reveals the Hebrews' concept that law is more than the mere Mosaic formulas and legal codes found in the Pentateuch. It includes the totality of all divine instruction and application.[22] Isaiah, particularly, used the word to underscore the divine nature of the inspired utterances spoken through him (see Isaiah 8:16, 20; 30:9–10), and Hosea used it for all those commandments, both ritual and ethical, which had been written down (Hosea 8:12). These early prophets understood *torah* as divine instructions, whether given by Moses, other prophets, or priests. All this emphasizes a point: it is not the form or agent that is objectively essential in *torah* but the divine authority that stands behind it.[23] The law was and is, at its very core, divine revelation.

The second fact the Bible teaches about the nature of law is that it is a treaty or covenant between God and His people. The outline of the Mosaic law follows the structure of ancient Near Eastern treaties between a suzerain and his people.[24] This underscores a point I have been making throughout this chapter. That is, what God gave Moses was more of a covenant treaty than it was a legal code. The Ten Commandments actually acted as a summary of the whole. The whole law was carved on two tables, not just one.[25] Each was a duplicate of the other, a copy for Israel and a copy for God.[26] Both were deposited in the Ark of the Covenant. This fits the ancient pattern of keeping important documents and valuable items in holy sanctuaries.

But to compare the law of Moses with others of the day does do it some injustice. It is unlike any of the half-dozen or so legal stelae archaeologists have found dating before or about the same time as Moses. These contain simply legal codes. God did not engrave a mere corpus of law on Moses' tables. They contained the covenant between God, the sovereign of heaven and earth, and His elect people, Israel.

To say it simply, the tables of Moses contained not law but covenant. Only that category can do justice to the revelation as a whole. The "ten words," as the Hebrew calls the Decalogue, act as *pars pro toto* (part for the whole), showing that the covenant is based on law and law keeping. Thus the Ten Commandments emphasize the type of covenant God created and formalized with Israel. The covenant declared God's lordship, but it also acted as a means by which people consecrated themselves to Him in a divinely dictated order of life.[27]

That last point needs to be emphasized. God is the sovereign holding all power over the earth. He gives His law to humankind as an act of sovereign grace by which He seeks to bind a people to Him. In this way the law becomes the token of Jehovah's electing power. Emphasizing this point, Moses taught his people:

> The Lord did not set his love upon you, nor choose you, because ye were more in number than any people; for ye were the fewest of all people:
> But because the Lord loved you, and because he would keep the oath which he had sworn unto your fathers, hath the Lord brought you out with a mighty hand, and redeemed you out of the house of bondmen, from the hand of Pharaoh king of Egypt (Deuteronomy 7:7–8).

However, God's election came with stipulations. "Know, therefore," Moses stressed, "that the Lord thy God, he is God, the faithful God, which keepeth covenant and mercy with them that love him and keep his commandments to a thousand generations" (Deuteronomy 7:9). Israel could therefore fully trust God as demonstrated by the fact that He redeemed them from slavery. This act alone proved that God would never break covenant. His *qânâ'* would not allow it. Thus, if it were broken, Israel would do the breaking. The consequences would be terrible. Indeed, the Lord "repayeth them that hate him to their face, to destroy them" (Deuteronomy 7:10). God's *qânâ'* would act as a two-edged sword that would work either for or against Israel, depending on their obedience or disobedience.

In this we see the purpose of the Ten Commandments. Those who willingly came under the law responded to the election offered by God. Obedience secured both the temporal and the eternal rewards.[28] Thus God gave His commandments not only for the guidance of His covenant people but also for a sign of their election. The Decalogue underscored Jehovah's election of Israel.[29] The law was designed to order both the inner and the outer life of His people. The holy calling and the final election could only be realized when both were in harmony.[30]

The third fact concerning the nature of biblical law or covenant is that it defines the plan for dominion *under God*. The command given to Adam was renewed with Noah after the Flood (see Genesis 9:1–17) and with each of the great patriarchs, and with Israel under Moses. Each of the prophets and kings also came under the law. Finally it was rearticulated by the Savior. In instituting the sacrament, He said, "This is my blood of the new testament" (Matthew 26:28). The word translated "testament" (Greek *diath*êkê) comes from the idea of making those arrangements necessary in order to facilitate agreements. Out of this came the notion of bonding or binding individuals or groups to one another. The one idea that takes in the whole range of meaning is *covenant*. Therefore, the Lord instituted with the sacrament the new covenant, but a covenant which did not do away with the old one, but rather fulfilled it through amplification. In this way, the sacrament reestablished God's law, but this time with a new elect group. The people of the new and everlasting covenant, now fully established in Christ, became the elect of God. These are they whom His atoning blood redeems and whom His grace calls to election in Him.[31]

Paul put it this way, "For this cause he [Christ] is the mediator of the new testament [*diath*êkê, covenant], that by means of death, for the redemption of the transgressions that were under the first testament [that is, the old covenant], they which are called might receive the promise of eternal inheritance" (Hebrews 9:15).

The picture that Paul paints is one of Christ's children inheriting His universal dominion as their eternal portion. The new testament, which expressed God's will for the newly elect, like that of any last will and testament, only came of force through the Savior's death.[32] But once it was in force, God's power and prerogatives were extended to the Saints. In this way, God's charge to Adam, to subdue the earth and exercise dominion over it under God's law, becomes the Saints'. They, in turn, were

recalled to the task of holding dominion over the earth and setting up God's kingdom through the privilege of their redemption
and election in Christ.[33] Due to apostasy, the early Church failed
in their responsibility.

God restored this law, and the responsibility to live it,
through Joseph Smith. The Book of Mormon contains all ten
commandments (see Mosiah 12:34–36; 13:12–24) and the Doctrine and Covenants restates nine. In this book of latter-day revelation, the Lord has made it clear that the Saints "should love and
serve him, the only living and true God" (D&C 20:19), that they
must see that "no idolatry nor wickedness [is] practiced" (D&C
52:39), and they must keep themselves "from evil to take the
name of the Lord in vain" (D&C 136:21). Further, they are to
"observe the Sabbath day to keep it holy" (D&C 68:29), to "love
thy neighbor as thyself, [and] shalt not steal; neither commit
adultery, nor kill, nor do anything like unto it" (D&C 59:6).
Finally, He commands, "Thou shalt not lie" (D&C 42:21), and,
"thou shalt not covet" (D&C 19:25). The only commandment
for which there is no reiteration in the Doctrine and Covenants is
"honor thy father and thy mother."

Latter-day scripture shows that the Lord has never annulled
these great commandments. They still form the ground of His
law code for the latter days and the base on which all covenants
stand. Keeping them continues to bring His grace upon His
people and acts as the means by which they show their acceptance
of that grace. We, like Israel of old, are called to build up God's
kingdom on earth and to prepare for Zion. As we live the Lord's
commandments, and the covenants they support, then shall our
God be close to us, and we shall become a great people and come
forth, "out of the wilderness—clear as the moon, and fair as the
sun, and terrible as an army with banners" (D&C 5:14).

Because so much rests on the base of the Ten Commandments, a detailed study of their meaning and importance for the
Latter-day Saints is in order. To that end this book is dedicated.

Notes

1. See Bruce R. McConkie, *Mormon Doctrine* (Salt Lake City: Bookcraft, 1966), 782–83.

2. For all words in this chapter translated from the Greek, see William F. Arndt and F. Wilbur Gingrich, *A Greek-English Lexicon of the New Testament and Other Early Christian Literature* (Chicago: University of Chicago Press, 1979).

3. The line comes from Walt Disney's *Mary Poppins.*

4. See Stephen E. Robinson, "The Law After Christ," *Ensign,* September 1983, 70.

5. *Webster's New Collegiate Dictionary,* s.v. "institute."

6. Ze'ev W. Falk, *Hebrew Law in Biblical Times* (Jerusalem, Israel: Wahrmann Books, 1964), 19–20.

7. Joseph Blenkinsopp, *Wisdom and Law in the Old Testament: the Ordering of Life in Israel and Early Judaism* (Oxford: Oxford University Press, 1995), 94–95.

8. Falk, *Hebrew Law,* 29–30.

9. Falk, *Hebrew Law,* 30.

10. The JST reads, "Whose name is Jehovah" rather than "Jealous." Still, the intent seems to be the same. Jehovah is a jealous God.

11. Dale Patrick, *Old Testament Law* (Atlanta: John Knox Press, 1985), 43.

12. Ibid., 43.

13. Ibid., 47.

14. Ibid.

15. Rousas John Rushdoony, *Institutes of Biblical Law* (n. c.: The Craig Press, 1973), 3.

16. Ibid.

17. Frances Brown, et. al., eds., *A Hebrew and English Lexicon of the Old Testament* (Oxford: Clarendon Press, 1953 reprint), s. v. *kâvâsh* and *râdâh.*

18. Hugh Nibley, "Man's Dominion," *New Era,* October 1972, 24–28.

19. Ibid.

20. Rushdoony, *Institutes,* 3.

21. Ernest F. Kevan, *The Moral Law* (Jenkintown, Pennsylvania: Sovereign Grace Publishers, 1963), 5–6.

22. Rushdoony, *Institutes,* 6.

23. Herman Kleinknecht and W. Gutbrod, *Law* (London: Adam and Charles Black, 1962), 21.

24. See Meredith G. Kline, *Treaty of the Great King, The Covenant Structure of Deuteronomy: Studies and Commentary* (Grand Rapids: Eerdmans, 1963), and J. A. Thompson, *The Ancient Near Eastern Treaties and the Old Testament* (London: the Tyndale Press, 1964).

25. Note that Exodus states "the tables were written on both their sides; on the one side and on the other were they written" (Exodus 32:15). This does not mean that both tables had writing on them, but that both tables had writing on the obverse *and* on the reverse. Each was full of writing.

26. Kline, *Treaty*, 19.

27. Ibid., 17.

28. Rushdoony, *Institutes*, 8.

29. Gustave Friedrich Oehler, *Theology of the Old Testament* (Grand Rapids: Zodervan, 1883), 177.

30. Rushdoony, *Institutes*, 8.

31. Alma 11:40; 1 Peter 1:2; Rushdoony, *Institutes*, 9.

32. Klein, *Treaty*, 41.

33. Rushdoony, *Institutes*, 9.

1

"Thou Shalt Have No Other Gods Before Me"

ROBERT J. MATTHEWS

HE TITLE OF THIS CHAPTER comes from Exodus 20:2–3 as the first of ten commandments given to Moses on Mount Sinai about three months after Israel's departure from Egypt. Although the exact year is not known, it was probably about 1490 B.C. It was a very dramatic occasion: The earth around Sinai shook, the Mount seemed engulfed with smoke and fire. Thunder rolled, and lightning streaked across the sky. Moses was high in the Mount in the midst of the activity. The people of Israel, near the foot of the Mount, felt the shaking, heard the thunder, saw the smoke, fire and lightning and withdrew to what they felt was a safe distance away. They also distinctly heard the voice of God speaking to Moses. (See Exodus 20:18; Deuteronomy 4:10–13, 33, 36.)

Robert J. Matthews served for eight years as dean of Religious Education at Brigham Young University. He is currently serving as president of the Mount Timpanogos Utah Temple. He and his wife, Shirley, are the parents of four children.

The Ten Commandments given through Moses to Israel formed the basis of an extensive legal system that regulated Israel throughout the period of the Old and New Testaments and also that of the Book of Mormon, and has since contributed to the legal systems of numerous civilized cultures.

We learn from latter-day revelation that, when first given to Moses, the Ten Commandments were accompanied by laws and ordinances of the Melchizedek Priesthood, and were an integral part of the plan of redemption, which is always associated with the fulness of the gospel of Jesus Christ. However, when most of Israel demonstrated that they were unwilling and spiritually unable to obey the fulness of the law of Christ, the Lord withdrew the ordinances of exaltation, which operate with the higher or Melchizedek Priesthood, and added in their place the lesser law of the Aaronic Priesthood, commonly known as the law of Moses. Both laws were of divine origin and both testify of the mission of Jesus Christ as the Holy One of Israel and the only true Messiah and Redeemer, but greater blessings attend the Melchizedek law. The Ten Commandments were contained in both instances (see JST Exodus 34:1–2; JST Deuteronomy 10:1–2; D&C 84:23–27; Galatians 3:19).

MAN'S RELATIONSHIP WITH GOD IS
OF FIRST IMPORTANCE

The sequence of the Ten Commandments—or the Decalogue, as they are sometimes called—is significant. At first glance it might seem that each command is a separate, independent statement, equally meaningful in any order, but a careful look shows a divine order. It will be noticed that the first four commandments pertain to our relationship to God: (1) Thou shalt have no other gods; (2) Thou shalt worship no graven images; (3) Thou shalt not take the name of God in vain; (4) Thou shalt honor God's holy Sabbath day. The remaining commandments pertain to relationships between individuals on earth: (5) Honor thy parents; (6) Thou shalt not kill; (7) Thou shalt not commit adultery; (8) Thou shalt not steal; (9) Thou shalt not bear false witness; (10) Thou shalt not covet anything that is thy neighbor's (see Exodus 20:2–17). The fifth commandment, which relates to parents, is a natural transition commandment between the two categories.

These two major areas, with statements pertaining to Deity being first, are apparent also in the order and sequence of the Beatitudes in the Sermon on the Mount delivered by Jesus to His twelve Apostles, especially as clarified in the Joseph Smith Translation (Matthew 5) and as presented in the Savior's sermon to the Nephites (3 Nephi 12), and also in the particular order of the Articles of Faith of The Church of Jesus Christ of Latter-day Saints, contained in the Pearl of Great Price. All of these instances are in complete accord with Jesus' pronouncement that the first great commandment of the law is to love the Lord God with all one's heart, and the second is to love one's neighbor as one's self (Matthew 22:35–40). Thus it is entirely proper and even necessary that the Ten Commandments should begin with a declaration concerning the supremacy of God: "I am the Lord thy God. . . . Thou shalt have no other gods before me."

Although the Exodus account is the earliest in our present Bibles in which the Ten Commandments are categorically stated, we are well aware that every principle inherent in them was known by the righteous patriarchs back to Adam, some 2500 years before Moses. Beginning with Adam, all the ancient worthies had the fulness of the gospel of Jesus Christ, including the higher or Melchizedek Priesthood and all the ordinances of exaltation and every law of righteousness later known to Moses and all the prophets. It is only in the structure of our current Bibles that the Ten Commandments appear first in Exodus 20. As an example of an earlier date, we find in Doctrine and Covenants 132:36 a declaration that in Abraham's day it was written, "Thou shalt not kill," which affirms a written code centuries before Exodus 20.

THE TRUE GOD OF HEAVEN AND EARTH

A major purpose of this chapter is to discuss the nature, character, and attributes of the God of Heaven, who is the God of Israel and God of the whole earth. It is not intended to argue for the existence of God; rather I have begun with the assumption that the reader already is a believer. The chapter proposes to describe briefly what the scriptures and the latter-day prophets tell us about God and how we can come to know Him. If we truly know Him we can distinguish between true doctrine and false notions about Him.

Worship Is Natural to Humans

Humans seem to have an inborn tendency and desire to worship something, almost anything—a display of strength or power; a supreme intelligence; a creator or father figure who they hope is benevolent, and so forth. The vast orderly universe, the wonders of nature, "mother earth," the intricacy of the human body, the depth of human psyche—each persuades some people that logically there must be a God. Intense feelings of worship and need for emotional and spiritual support often rise to the surface of consciousness during prolonged periods of stress and serious trouble, terminal illness, death of loved ones, or even one's own old age. Such is evidenced in the cultural music or "spirituals" of the black African slaves in early America, where their hope and trust in redemption through Jesus is sorrowfully expressed.

Since it does seem natural for mankind to worship something, it appears to me that people have to be taught in order to become atheists or infidels. Lost childhood innocence and natural trust are replaced by cynicism, skepticism, and doubt as learned responses. This may have been what Paul referred to when he wrote to the Colossian Saints: "Beware lest any man spoil you through philosophy and vain deceit, after the tradition of men, after the rudiments of the world, and not after Christ" (Colossians 2:8).

The scriptures were written so that man might have hope and be comforted (see Romans 15:4) and that "whoso believeth in God might with surety hope for a better world, yea, even a place at the right hand of God, which hope cometh of faith [and] maketh an anchor to the souls of men" (Ether 12:4).

Correct Knowledge Necessary for Faith

In the early days of The Church of Jesus Christ of Latter-day Saints a series of seven doctrinal lectures was prepared under the direction of the First Presidency for the purpose of instructing the elders and other members in the important subject of faith in God. These lectures, now called *Lectures on Faith,* were delivered orally in Kirtland, Ohio, in the winter of 1834–35 and later were for a time included in the Doctrine and Covenants. The basic subject was the nature of God, the text declaring at great length that unless a person has a correct idea of God he cannot exercise strong faith in Him. The lectures follow an orderly and progressive plan,[1] discussing among other things the following:

— How the idea that there is a God was first planted in the mind of man. It was by God revealing himself to Adam. (Lecture 2.)
— The object on which true faith unto life and salvation rests. It is on a correct knowledge of the character and attributes of God. (Lecture 3.)
— Six attributes of God are: knowledge, power, justice, judgment, mercy, and truth. In each of these God is perfect, supreme, and unchanging, lacking nothing. (Lectures 3 and 4.)
— The matchless power, majesty, and unity of the three persons of the Godhead. All who have true faith will receive power to become like the Godhead. (Lecture 5.)

The foregoing deals with the first five lectures; lectures 6 and 7 will be summarized later in this discussion.

A major and oft-repeated topic of the lectures is that these concepts and ideas about God can only be known if God reveals himself. Without direct revelation mankind has only opinion and guesswork, which are inefficient to enable the mind of a rational person to develop true faith.

In successive years the Prophet Joseph Smith gave additional information about what God is. On April 2, 1843, the Prophet said: "The Father has a body of flesh and bones as tangible as man's; the Son also; but the Holy Ghost has not a body of flesh and bones, but is a personage of Spirit" (D&C 130:22).

On 7 April 1844 in a funeral address popularly known as the King Follett Discourse, the Prophet is reported to have said:

God himself was once as we are now, and is an exalted man, and sits enthroned in yonder heavens! That is the great secret. If the veil were rent today, and the great God who holds this world in its orbit, and who upholds all worlds and all things by his power, was to make himself visible,—I say, if you were to see him today, you would see him like a man in form—like yourselves in all the person, image, and very form as a man; for Adam was created in the very fashion, image and likeness of God, and received instruction from, and walked, talked and conversed with him, as one man talks and communes with another. . . .

These are incomprehensible ideas to some, but they are simple. It is the first principle of the Gospel to know for a certainty the Character of God, and to know that we may converse with him as one man converses with another, and that he was once a man like us; yea, that God himself, the Father of us all, dwelt on an earth, the same as Jesus Christ himself did; and I will show it from the Bible.[2]

A very important aspect of Deity is that He is holy. He is not capricious, or malicious, or crafty, but He is holy. Since He is holy He requires His children to be holy. We read in Leviticus 11:44: "For I am the Lord your God: ye shall therefore sanctify yourselves, and ye shall be holy; for I am holy." Indeed, one of His titles is the "Holy One of Israel" (see 2 Nephi 25:29).

GOD IS KNOWN ONLY BY REVELATION

The truths about Deity presented in this chapter are deep and ponderous and are known in the Church only because of revelation to the Prophet Joseph Smith and his prophetic associates. The Prophet emphasized the need for revelation: "We never can comprehend the things of God and of heaven, but by revelation. We may spiritualize and express opinions to all eternity; but that is no authority."[3]

Again from the Prophet Joseph:

If it requires the Spirit of God to know the things of God; and the spirit of the devil can only be unmasked through that medium, then it follows as a natural consequence that unless some person or persons have a communication, or revelation from God, unfolding to them the operation of the spirit, they must eternally remain ignorant of these principles; for I contend that if one man cannot understand these things but by the Spirit of God, ten thousand men cannot; it is alike out of the reach of the wisdom of the learned, the tongue of the eloquent, the power of the mighty. And we shall at last have to come to this conclusion, whatever we may think of revelation, that without it we can neither know nor understand anything of God, or the devil.[4]

With revelation being the one and only way for mankind to know anything with certitude about Deity, it follows that in the absence of revelation the human family doesn't know—indeed, cannot know—whether their beliefs and notions about God are true or false.

We thus learn some basic truths about the nature, character, and fatherliness of God our Heavenly Parent. He is everything to us. We owe Him our total and complete undivided allegiance and

worship. The commandment states, "Thou shalt have no other
gods before me." When this was spoken to ancient Israel they
were just out of Egypt, where they had been exposed to many
gods of wood and stone. The commandment could be read in
such a way as to mean: "You may have other gods, but do not put
them ahead of or above me," but such an interpretation would be
completely contrary to all else we know about true worship. The
only allowable meaning has to be: "I am the Lord thy God. . . .
Thou shalt have no other gods at all—none whatsoever—period!"

FALSE GODS

A false god could be defined as anything that detracts us from
the worship and service to the true God. In some cultures idols of
wood or stone are objects of adoration, veneration, and worship.
The Lord Jehovah pointed to the irrationality of worshiping a
man-made idol with this example: A man cuts down a tree; with
part he shapes an idol god to worship; with another part he
kindles a fire to cook his food. In the end, He says, both parts
will turn to ashes (see Isaiah 44:9–20).[5]

So prevalent was the worship of idols in Isaiah's day that
chapters 40–47 of his record are directed primarily to showing
the superiority of Jehovah, Israel's God, to the dumb, inanimate
know-nothing idols. Israel's God can foretell the future, and is
the creator of earth and man and the heavens, and so forth.

Material Possessions Are Often a Substitute God

Not all idol worship is confined to primitive religious cere-
monies in faraway lands and ancient cultures such as Egypt,
Canaan and Babylon. The Lord has warned us against another
form of idol worship, one that is every bit as real and as spiritually
destructive as that which was common in the ancient biblical
world. Current idol worship is found in the tendency of humans
to place their trust in, and focus their chief interest in obtaining,
material things—money, property, riches, which generally bring

political power, secular learning, and social influence. The Lord has warned us about the materialism of modern Babylon: "They seek not the Lord to establish his righteousness, but every man walketh in his own way, and after the image of his own god, whose image is in the likeness of the world, and whose substance is that of an idol, which waxeth old and shall perish in Babylon, even Babylon the great, which shall fall" (D&C 1:16).

The great Apostle Paul confronted the same flaws in human character in his day. He wrote against the indulgence of physical appetites and an over-concern with self-importance and worldly influences. We find the following in Paul's writings in the New Testament: Of those who "mind earthly things," he said, their "God is their belly" (Philippians 3:19). They "serve not our Lord Jesus Christ, but their own belly" (Romans 16:18).

Of those who had become obsessed with the possession of physical things, which are perishable, and which had caused them to lose their focus on the everlasting and imperishable God, Paul spoke of their "vain imaginations," their "foolish heart," and said that they "served the creature more than the Creator" (Romans 1:21, 25).

Jesus addressed the proclivity of mankind to slip into the false security of materialism when he spoke of the "deceitfulness of riches" (Matthew 13:22), and also when He declared that "no servant can serve two masters" such as God and mammon (Luke 16:13). "Mammon" is not simply worldly wealth, but the lust and greed for it, and the lusts of the flesh that accompany the life of the natural man. In other words, no man can wholeheartedly serve God if at the same time he nurtures a greed for worldly fame, riches, and lusts of the flesh. Furthermore, when the Brethren returned to their fishing nets Jesus chided Peter with the question: "Lovest thou me more than these?" (John 21:15). Jesus expressed the fundamental, underlying principle when He said: "For where your treasure is, there will your heart be also" (Matthew 6:21).

The propensity is so strong for man to gravitate toward excessive attachment to physical things close at hand, and to place affection on and become emotionally dependent upon other human beings, that the Prophet Joseph Smith gave this counsel in a funeral address in 1842: "When we lose a near and dear friend, upon whom we have set our hearts, it should be a caution unto us not to set our affections too firmly upon others, knowing that they may in like manner be taken from us. Our affections should be placed upon God and His work, more intensely than upon our fellow beings."[6] In giving such advice, the Prophet echoed Paul's words, "Set your affection on things above, not on things on the earth" (Colossians 3:2).

Even many who might profess no religion per se go about their secular activation with religious zeal and commitment. The English word *religion* comes from the Latin *religio* which is associated with the word *liga-ment*, meaning "band" or "tie," as in the manner muscles and cords are tied to bones in a body. Our religion, so to speak, ties us emotionally and spiritually to things. True religion ties us to God; false religion ties us to less worthy idol-types of things. Thus those who profess atheism or agnosticism seem tied to their personal views. A religion without God as its focal point may actually be a religion with man as the center of adoration, or it may focus on philosophy, or science, or law, or government. Today in the United States, when mention of God is banned from public school and government discourse, we have seen the growth and development of what is tantamount to a "civil religion" that has zealot-like adherents and proponents. A civil religion is replacing the religion of faith and personal morality that had its focus on the God of heaven. It is in reality a secular state religion, a godless substitute for the revealed religion of the scriptures.[7]

The False Gods People Worship

In a colorful and highly expressive manner Elder Orson Pratt spoke his views about false gods in a pamphlet published in the British Isles in 1848.[8] Following are brief excerpts from a lengthy treatise on the nature of God:

There have been various species of idolatry in different ages of the world. The sun, moon, stars, beasts, crocodiles, frightful serpents, images of wood, of stone, and of brass, have been erected into gods, and worshiped by innumerable multitudes. But the system of idolatry, invented by modern Christianity, far surpasses in absurdity anything that we have ever heard of.

They have introduced a God without body, parts or passions. They have had the audacity to call this newly-invented god by the same name as the God of the ancient saints, although there is not the least resemblance between them. Indeed there could be no resemblance between them; for a bodiless god, without parts or passions, could resemble nothing in heaven, on earth, or in hell. This imaginary modern god has become exceedingly popular.

Elder Pratt reasoned that the description of such a god was actually a description of "nothing." Only nothing has no parts, no passions, no material substance; consequently, it could not have an image, either a moral or the physical image after which man was created. He concluded that a definition of such a god was essentially "a pious name for Atheism." Some may find his words offensive, however, they are a logical interpretation of the written creeds of historic Christianity from the fourth century onward.

Elder Pratt's reasoning is that if the God of heaven existed only as He is declared to exist in various creeds of Christendom— that is uncreated, immaterial, without body, parts, or passions— He could not be an actual, live, conscious, loving being. Continuing from Elder Pratt:

The true God exists both in time and in space, and has as much relation to them as man or any other being. He has extension, and form, and dimensions, as well as man. He occupies space; has a body, parts, and passions; can go from place to place—can eat, drink and talk, as well as man. Man resembles Him in the features and form of his body, and he does not differ materially in size.

In 1976 President Spencer W. Kimball, being much concerned about the lifestyle of many persons—even members of the true Church who have a more correct understanding of God and of eternity than the world in general—beautifully and compassionately warned of the obvious erosion to faith that is manifest in an over-dependence on and excessive desire for material wealth to be used for selfish purposes. This he described as an "ever deepening idolatry." President Kimball wrote:

> I use the word *idolatry* intentionally. As I study ancient scripture, I am more and more convinced that there is significance in the fact that the commandment "Thou shalt have no other gods before me" is the first of the Ten Commandments.
>
> Few men have ever knowingly and deliberately chosen to reject God and his blessings. Rather, we learn from the scriptures that because the exercise of faith has always appeared to be more difficult than relying on things more immediately at hand, carnal man has tended to transfer his trust in God to material things. Therefore, in all ages when men have fallen under the power of Satan and lost the faith, they have put in its place a hope in the "arm of flesh" and in "gods of silver, and gold, of brass, iron, wood, and stone, which see not, nor hear, nor know" (Daniel 5:23)—that is, in idols. This I find to be a dominant theme in the Old Testament. Whatever thing a man sets his heart and his trust in most is his god; and if his god doesn't also happen to be the true and living God of Israel, that man is laboring in idolatry.

In speaking of the luxury and unprecedented wealth of many today, President Kimball asked:

Do we have more of these good things than our faith can stand? Many people spend most of their time working in the service of a self-image that includes sufficient money, stocks, bonds, investment portfolios, property, credit cards, furnishings, automobiles, and the like to *guarantee* carnal security throughout, it is hoped, a long and happy life. Forgotten is the fact that our assignment is to use these many resources in our families and quorums to build up the kingdom of God— to further the missionary effort and the genealogical and temple work; to raise our children up as fruitful servants unto the Lord; to bless others in every way, that they may also be fruitful. Instead, we expend these blessings on our own desires.

In spite of our delight in defining ourselves as modern, and our tendency to think we possess a sophistication that no people in the past ever had—in spite of these things, we are, on the whole, an idolatrous people—a condition most repugnant to the Lord.

President Kimball expressed his sadness that we put our trust in military weapons of war instead of in God and in His protection. He concluded with this advice:

> We must leave off the worship of modern-day idols and a reliance on the "arm of flesh," for the Lord has said to all the world in our day, "I will not spare any that remain in Babylon." (D&C 64:24.)[9]

One evidence of the shift toward a materialistic society is the commercialism associated with Christmas. A *Deseret News* article reported the findings of the Barna Research Group, Ltd., of Oxnard, California, which discovered that of 1006 adults surveyed in July 1996, only 37 per cent said that the birth of Jesus was for them the most important aspect of Christmas. The report said that older respondents were more likely to associate Jesus with Christmas than were younger people. The article also said that "Americans are more likely to correctly recall the significance of April 15 [income tax deadline] than they are to connect Christmas with the birth of Jesus. As America becomes increasingly anesthetized to Christian principles and practices, it seems only fitting that we have contracted acute amnesia regarding the spiritual significance of December 25."[10]

IMPORTANCE OF KNOWING AND OBEYING THE TRUE GOD

The importance of worshiping and knowing the true God of heaven can be summarized succinctly. In prayer to the Father, Jesus said: "And this is life eternal, that they might know thee the only true God, and Jesus Christ, whom thou hast sent" (John 17:3). We quickly sense that it is one thing to know about God, and a much larger thing to *know* Him. Jesus said it is necessary to *know* God, not just know of Him. Even the devil knows that there is a God, but such knowledge will not save him (see James 2:19). Furthermore, it is one thing to know that there is a heaven. It is yet another thing to know for certain that one is going there. It is actually little comfort to know that there is a God and a heaven unless we also have some hope and assurance that we are going to be there.

Earlier in this discussion, reference was made to *Lectures on Faith*. The first five lectures deal with the nature of faith and what kind of a being God is, so that a rational person can place faith in Him. The sixth lecture explains that in addition to knowing there is a God, and knowing what His character and attributes are, a third qualification is necessary. Through faith one renders willing obedience to God in keeping the specific commandments He has given man. When that occurs, the individual obtains a testimony that his or her life is acceptable to the will of God. Such status can be obtained only by unmixed faith and devotion to the true God. The price is high—a willingness to sacrifice all things for the gospel of Jesus Christ. These words are found in Lecture 6:7, 10, 12:

7. Let us here observe, that a religion that does not require the sacrifice of all things never has power sufficient to produce the faith necessary unto life and salvation; for, from the first existence of man, the faith necessary unto the enjoyment of life and salvation never could be obtained without the sacrifice of all earthly things. It was through this sacrifice, and this only, that God has ordained that men should enjoy eternal life; and it is through the medium of the sacrifice of all earthly things that men do actually know that they are doing the things that are well pleasing in the sight of God.

10. Those, then, who make the sacrifice, will have the testimony that their course is pleasing in the sight of God; and those who have this testimony will have faith to lay hold on eternal life, and will be enabled, through faith, to endure unto the end, and receive the crown that is laid up for them that love the appearing of our Lord Jesus Christ. But those who do not make the sacrifice cannot enjoy this faith, because men are dependent upon this sacrifice in order to obtain this faith; therefore, they cannot lay hold upon eternal life, because the revelations of God do not guarantee unto them the authority so to do, and without this guarantee faith could not exist.

12. But those who have not made this sacrifice to God do not know that the course which they pursue is well pleasing in his sight; for whatever may be their belief or their opinion, it is a matter of doubt and uncertainty in their mind; and where doubt and uncertainty are there faith is not, nor can it be. For doubt and faith do not exist in the same person at the same time.[11]

The seventh lecture describes the results that always flow from true faith. Since Jesus and the Father are the prototypes or perfect examples of saved beings, all who become saved in the future will become as they are.

Obviously no one reaches this high condition of perfection without a proper concept and a fully determined life of voluntary obedience to the true and living God. The process begins by one's learning who and what the true God is. That knowledge is then followed by obedience made possible by faith.

While it is from the Bible that we learn of the Ten Commandments, it is only through the atonement and resurrection of Jesus Christ that salvation is possible. And it is only through the Prophet Joseph Smith and present living prophets and Apostles that we in this day have access to God through the authority of the Holy Priesthood, and the ordinances, and the correct perspective about God.

Notes

1. The full text of *Lectures on Faith* can be found in any edition of the Doctrine and Covenants from 1835 until they were removed in 1921. The lectures have been published separately by both Bookcraft and Deseret Book, publishers in Salt Lake City, and by the Religious Studies Center of BYU in 1990.

2. Joseph Fielding Smith, comp., *Teachings of the Prophet Joseph Smith* (Salt Lake City: Deseret Book, 1976), 345–46. Hereinafter identified as *TPJS*.

3. *TPJS*, 292.

4. *TPJS*, 205.

5. A similar concept is found in the apocryphal work, "Revelation of Abraham," *Improvement Era* 1:705–14 (August 1898). This account is apparently not from Abraham, but is regarded by textual scholars as having originated in the first century A.D.

6. *TPJS*, 216.

7. An informative treatise on the role of "civil religion" in modern society is found in James E. Faust, "A New Civil Religion," *Finding Light in a Dark World* (Salt Lake City: Deseret Book, 1995), 59–68.

8. The excerpts used herein are from "The Kingdom of God," *Orson Pratt's Works*, vol. 1 (Liverpool: 1848). Reprinted by Parker Pratt Robison (Salt Lake City: Deseret News Press, 1945), 35, 36.

9. "The False Gods We Worship," *Ensign*, June 1976, 4–6.

10. David Briggs, "Holiday Poll Confirms Clergy's Fears," *Deseret News*, B–6, November 30, 1996.

11. *Lectures on Faith*, 6: 7, 10, 12.

2

"Thou Shalt Not Make unto Thee Any Graven Image"

S. BRENT FARLEY

*A*T FIRST GLANCE IT WOULD seem that of all the Ten Commandments this one would be of least concern to those of modern times. Not so, however. It is probably one of the most frequently violated of the Ten Commandments, Latter-day Saints not excepted.

An "image" is a reproduction of the appearance or likeness of someone or something. We are informed that "God created man in his own image, in the image of God created he him; male and female created he them" (Genesis 1:27). Our bodies and spirits are in the image of God.

A basic theme from a well-known Primary hymn teaches what image is proper to seek:

S. Brent Farley is director of the Logan Institute of Religion and conducts the institute show choir, "New Horizons." He is the author of Missionary Feelings *and* Spiritually Yours. *He and his wife, Janene, are the parents of six children.*

"I am a child of God, and he has sent me here;
Has given me an earthly home, with parents kind and dear.
Lead me, guide me, walk beside me, help me find the way;
Teach me all that I must do, to live with him someday."[1]

Sung in Primary, this inspired musical text provides a foundation for an understanding of the second commandment: "Thou shalt not make unto thee any graven image" (Exodus 20:4). The children sing "I am a child of God." We literally *are* children of God. As Marion G. Romney stated: "The spirits of men 'are begotten sons and daughters unto God' (D&C 76:24). Through that birth process, self-existing intelligence was organized into individual spirit beings."[2]

God knows our potential, the end possibilities of our eternal destiny. We have the opportunity to seek our greatest potential by developing spiritually until we have "the image of God engraven upon [our] countenances" (Alma 5:19). That is a spiritual gift, qualified for by faithfulness and received through the kindly grace of God. That is the only proper image we may seek. As long as we recognize our divine parentage and receive an "engraving" of God's characteristics upon our own souls, line upon line and precept upon precept (see D&C 98:12), we are on the "right track." God is willing to make of us divine individuals.

Unfortunately, because of the necessary "opposition in all things" (2 Nephi 2:11), many of us fall to the temptations and uncertainties fostered by Satan: we try to make images and gods to ourselves, and sometimes (falsely so) *of* ourselves.

In ancient Israel some would carve, sculpt, and molten, transforming wood, stone, and metals to bear the image and label of a "god." For example, "the workman melteth a graven image, and the goldsmith spreadeth it over with gold, and casteth silver chains" (Isaiah 40:19). This was carried from place to place, set up by mortal hands, and worshipped as a god.

It was a fairly safe concept, or so it seemed, because the god was dependent upon the man or woman who owned and transported it. It could require nothing, could not judge or punish, and could not interact with its maker, though one could ask anything of it one desired and superstitiously hope for a fulfillment. It could not see, hear, talk, touch, feel, or move. Jehovah reasoned the foolishness of cutting down a tree, using part for the warmth of a fire, part to cook on, "and the residue thereof he maketh a god, even his graven image: he falleth down unto it, and worshippeth it, and prayeth unto it, and saith, Deliver me; for thou art my god" (Isaiah 44:16–17).

To create such an object of worship was a direct violation of both the first commandment, "Thou shalt have no other gods before me," and the second, "Thou shalt not make unto thee any graven image" (Exodus 20:3, 4). One is inseparably connected with the other. Choosing another god or an image of such constitutes apostasy from the truth we knew in the premortal existence: it is a sin that leads away from exaltation.

Antiquity does not contain the only violators of the second commandment. There are still in the world today individuals who build an image and devote their religious affinities to that object. Elder Russell M. Nelson has written:

> Is this commandment still relevant in our day? It most certainly is. In one country I visited recently, for example, people kneel in worship before an object of their own creation. It has the body of a man and the head of an elephant. They call him Lord (Ganesh) and pray to him. In fact, in many of the most populous and poverty-stricken nations of the earth, images and statuary constitute the object of adoration of people in ignorance of this great second commandment. Their disobedience keeps them from the blessings of prosperity that God has promised to his faithful children.[3]

Lest we be too quick to condemn, however, we ought to consider the possibility that many who worship "ignorantly," as Paul said (Acts 17:23), may ofttimes be yielding to that premortal magnetism which attracts a human being to his Heavenly Father. We have an innate desire to build a relationship with God.

Brigham Young explained:

> The existence of a Supreme Being is universally acknowl-
> edged by man. This is to be found in the lowest of the hea-
> then nations, and they worship according to the best knowl-
> edge they have. The inhabitants of Hindostan, Japan, &c., are
> devotional people, though they worship before images, not
> knowing better. The aborigines of this country also worship
> according to their traditions, as do all the heathen nations.
> They make their graven images of brass, wood, silver, and
> gold to represent the Deity they seek to please. . . . But ask
> them if they worship these pictures and images, and they will
> tell you, "No: the picture or image only represents to the eye
> the Being we worship." So it is with the worship of the hea-
> then nations: they will tell you they "do not worship the inan-
> imate image, but that the God they worship is in eternity. We
> do not see him, but our fathers have taught us many things
> which we wish to retain in memory. . . ." Then do not depre-
> ciate the heathen worship, nor the brethren of our former
> Christian faith; for the majority of them worship according to
> the best knowledge they have.[4]

Those who do indeed worship according to the best knowledge they have, if they are honest and truth-seeking, will gain
greater knowledge as they yield to the promptings of the light of
Christ. This in turn will lead eventually to a witness from the
Holy Ghost of the true God and His church (see D&C
84:46–48).

Referring to the concept of false gods and graven images
since the Creation, Elder Bernard P. Brockbank said that "billions
through the centuries including the very elect have been deceived
and misled."[5]

President Spencer W. Kimball testified that when we liken the
scriptures to ourselves "we will see many parallels between the
ancient worship of graven images and behavioral patterns in our
very own experience." He explained that "whatever thing a man

sets his heart and his trust in most is his god: and if his god doesn't also happen to be the true and living God of Israel, that man is laboring in idolatry."[6]

In a museum in New Zealand I viewed the graven image of an ancient false god. It was made of thin metal shaped like a human head and chest. It had jewels for eyes, something unidentifiable for an approximation of hair on the head, and the upper torso had an extension to resemble an arm and a hand. According to the plaque beneath this object, specified body parts from the sacrificial human victim were placed in the metal hand as part of a ritual. I thought to myself, "How ridiculous to sacrifice human life to this object that could literally be crunched and thrown into a trash can! How could anyone do something like that?" Yet, apparently, many people had. It is difficult to imagine something like that occurring today in a modern-world setting. Yet the graven images of our own time draw such devotion from such masses of people as to be almost shocking. It's just that the modern graven images are designed more attractively (and are less recognizable as graven images) than the museum model I saw.

Consider, for example, the slender, rounded graven images of paper filled with tobacco, readily available in a variety of commercial establishments, the addictive and harmful smoke ready to contribute to the modern sacrifice of human body parts. Cigars and cigarettes are neatly packaged and heavily advertised; their sacrificial victims often come willingly and even pay money to participate in this smoking ritual.

Did you ever notice the variety of shapes, sizes, and colors of containers holding the graven image of alcoholic beverages? Rather than being tucked away in a museum, they are displayed in attractive and cleverly designed advertisements to draw intelligent people to offer themselves up in a sacrifice that costs thousands of lives, marriages, and families annually. Is this any less ridiculous than the museum model? Not many view alcoholic beverages as the powerful and deceptive graven images that they are.

Drug abuse is another issue: potentially helpful substances for treatment of illnesses can be turned into graven images as horrible as the ancient images shaped for the sacrifice of living persons.

One of the most commonly used graven images of our time is an electronic model: it brings a myriad of sights and sounds into the home and is controlled by a remote device so convenient that one doesn't even have to stand up to change the display. While not a graven image to everyone, a television can become so when it begins to exercise control over the viewer, and not vice versa. When the controller becomes the controlled, idolatry is near.

There are many graven images that are not made of a substance but of a concept (thus being more difficult to detect). Consider, for example, the images of popularity, wealth, and power graven in the hearts and minds of many. Do you want a specific example close to home? How many children are threatened with loss of popularity and friends if they don't dress in the current model of clothing or shoes that designers herald as the best "image maker"? How many adults themselves worship that image for their children, along with the "grown up" graven images of fashion?

In the business world can sales charts and networking lines become graven images of worship? Can a clock or a daily planner extend beyond its usefulness to the status of a controlling graven image? Is the stock market a powerful graven image in the lives of many investors? For politicians, how many times does the "poll of popularity" flash as a graven image of polished gold? Perhaps, when properly understood, the second commandment is not very old-fashioned at all, but is every bit as relevant to us in our day as to the ancient Israelites in theirs.

With a wandering gaze and lustful thoughts, is it possible, like David of old, to allow a beautiful woman married to someone else to become one's graven image of adoration? What greater image of worship than the false god of sex, with its multitudinous variety of supporting images in magazines, movies, audios, stores, and on computer networks?

Do I dare suggest the "graven image" possibilities contained in the world of sports? How important is a WIN; the need for "do or die" competitiveness; the superimposition of THE GAME over anything else on the weekly schedule; the NEED for a particular brand of shoe to achieve maximum efficiency? And how about the "hero-worshipping" mentality that is constantly heaped upon the altars belonging to the star players?

As with sports, so with music. What could be good and beautiful is misused by Satan with a distortion of sound and beat, forming a graven image like "the noise of [Satan's] viols" (Isaiah 14:11). As a graven image, bad music has become a medium for the selling of evil disguised in the robes of popularity.

Modern conveniences have simplified and improved our lives immeasurably. When our appreciation turns to devotion, however, and our efforts to own things for their own worth and not the good they can do for others alters our sense of values, then we slip again into the realm of modern graven images.

President Kimball explained:

> The Lord has blessed us as a people with a prosperity unequaled in times past. The resources that have been placed in our power are good, and necessary to our work here on the earth. But I am afraid that many of us have been surfeited with flocks and herds and acres and barns and wealth and have begun to worship them as false gods, and they have power over us. Do we have more of these good things than our faith can stand? Many people spend most of their time working in the service of a self-image that includes sufficient money, stocks. bonds, investment portfolios, property, credit cards, furnishings, automobiles, and the like to *guarantee* carnal security throughout, it is hoped, a long and happy life. Forgotten is the fact that our assignment is to use these many resources in our families and quorums to build up the kingdom of God—to further the missionary effort and the genealogical and temple work; to raise our children up as fruitful servants unto the Lord; to bless others in every way, that they may also be fruitful. Instead, we expend these blessings on our own desires.[7]

Some graven images that we create to ourselves are like large pendants hung about the neck, glittering in the light for anyone to see. Others may be small and far less noticeable, winking on occasion when the light catches them "just right." It may not be that the activity, philosophy, or other pursuits which become graven images were inherently evil: rather, it is probably the inordinate light in which they are held and the inappropriate degree of commitment that makes of them a violation of the second commandment. Sexual relations, for example, are the foundation for life. The earth's purpose could never be achieved if continuing generations of children were not born. But outside of the Lord's purposes and inside the domains of Satan sex becomes one of the worst of evil images, mirrored by the media to the masses.

Money builds the Lord's kingdom in righteousness, and monetary contributions can bring the blessings of heaven in ways unequaled by personal material gain. As a graven image, however, money can destroy souls, cities, and kingdoms. (Have you ever thought of a lottery ticket as a graven image?). Gambling casinos are adorned with brightly colored graven images ready to accept the sacrifices of their worshippers.

Images of gold, silver, and precious gems often adorn our bodies in the form of jewelry. Does this imply that jewelry is bad and that the wearer is a transgressor? It depends upon the motive of the wearer and the investment of attention toward the jewelry as an object. For example, the wedding ring is an accepted symbol of love and commitment in a marriage relationship. The object represents a pure motive that suggests good. It does not draw attention to itself (excuse the excitement of the newly engaged who usually and appropriately herald such attention) as much as it suggests a relationship of love. Thus, it is not a graven image. But it could be if too much attention, show, and self-worth is attached to the symbol of love. On a larger scale, the owners (and dealers) of jewelry stores often make graven images of their wares when they try to teach that true love is manifested by the jewelry given. The implied logic is that if a man loves someone, he will give her jewelry, and by that gift she will then know the depth of his love. (Conversely, the implication is that the less expensive jewelry represents a lesser degree of love.) The object is thus placed above the principle and falsely represents it. (Needless to say, the more jewelry sold in the name of love the greater the profits to the jewelers.) Do the advertisers ever consider that they may be depicting images of idolatry in their advertisements?

Is jewelry in general bad, then? In complementing the attractiveness of an individual, moderate jewelry may have its place. But what if one begins to love jewelry for its "showiness"? What if one begins to look down on those who cannot afford to be as ornately decorated as others are? If one begins to judge the worth of self and others by the possession of fine jewelry, one is forming a graven image as real as the golden calf of ancient Israel.

What jewels would impress the Lord? Not objects, but righteous people: "And they shall be mine, saith the Lord of Hosts, in that day when I make up my jewels" (3 Nephi 24:17). It is the balance of priority between objects and individuals that determines appropriateness.

As with jewelry, so with apparel. The ancient Nephites were warned by the prophet Jacob:

> Because some of you have obtained more abundantly than that of your brethren ye are lifted up in the pride of your hearts, and wear stiff necks and high heads because of the costliness of your apparel, and persecute your brethren because ye suppose that ye are better than they.
>
> And now, my brethren, do ye suppose that God justifieth you in this thing? Behold, I say unto you, Nay. But he condemneth you, and if ye persist in these things his judgments must speedily come unto you. (Jacob 2:13–14.)

Nephi prophesied that the same problem would exist in our day (see 2 Nephi 28:13–14). Many (both in and out of the Lord's church) who would never bow down to a god of wood or stone kneel quickly before the graven images of fine or popular clothing. The advertisers broadcast their graven images of apparel throughout the world, casting for sales like a fisherman for fish.

Another topic: automobiles. They are wonderful means of transportation, a necessary luxury in many parts of the world. When do they cruise into the realm of graven images? Almost any time you watch a commercial describing them. Imagine the ancient Israelites gazing not upon a golden calf but upon a modern sports car on a pedestal of stone. A graven image on wheels! What an impressive idol that would have been (especially if they had started the engine and placed it in gear). When is it a nice commodity and when is it a graven image? That all depends upon the owner and his motives. Graven images are often parked in out-of-the-way places, or kitty-corner in two spaces so as to avoid unsightly scratches and dents (for a price, insurance companies will insure the repairability of the graven image).

How many homes fall within the category of graven images? That again depends upon the motives of the owners. How many are designed primarily to be bigger and better and more showy than the others around them? How many houses are credits to the skilled craftsmanship of the builders of modern-day graven images? Again, what is the purpose served in one's view of the home? Is it status and prestige? Is a family in an expensive home more valuable than a family in a modest or very poor one? Do we center our work motives toward the purchase of an expensive home in order to ensure our self-worth over others less well-to-do? Perhaps we need to look again at our motives as we invest them in material possessions.

In the professional world, can a resume receive just a little too much polish, being overlaid with the silver of arrogance and the gold of pride? If so, another graven image has been created by the hands of man.

Do the writers' and teachers' needs or desires to publish ever cross the bounds of service into the realm of false worship? To the book distributors of today, who would care anyway? The golden image of the cash register will proclaim the success of the sales, one graven image complementing the other. It is not that books and articles are bad; to the contrary, they can be wonderful. But when they become objects of gain more than of service, the shadow of idolatry creeps closer. And what about the lecturers? Are they serving mankind in a meaningful way or serving themselves as graven images of popularity? Many television preachers and news media representatives ought to ask themselves that question!

Graven images have made some serious inroads into the lives of many in the Church. Numberless cases that involve Church disciplinary councils have been notched in the base of the giant graven image of sexual gratification. In addition, the image of power and control has been revered by domineering husbands and fathers to such a degree that questions regarding worthiness in the Church now necessitate a reference to abuse (also asked of the sisters).

There is another, more subtle graven image among Church members that often brings sorrow and loss of self-worth to faithful Latter-day-Saint parents who have rebellious or wayward children. It is the graven image of a "perfect family," the ideal structure representing the ideal Latter-day-Saint setting. This graven image does not allow for failure or agency; it demands that every child in an active Latter-day-Saint home be a model child. It cries that those parents who have children breaking the commandments of the Lord must hang their heads in shame. It requires that such parents consider themselves as failures; that they take the blame for the wrong choices of their children. It urges such parents to avoid the gaze of others who have (or seem to have) children better than theirs. To those parents fortunate enough to have all of their children active, serving missions, and marrying in temples, this graven image often tempts to look down on (or pity) their brothers and sisters who do not enjoy the same peace they do. It also whispers the taunt that those parents were not as good in their parenting as those without similar problems: "If they were *my* children, they wouldn't have gotten away with that!" As with other graven images, the worship of this falsity brings unhappiness and hinders progress.

While the perfect family is the ultimate goal of the gospel, it must be chosen by the various members of the family in order to be achieved. Even our Heavenly Father had rebellious children in the premortal existence, and still does today. Like Him, we ought to continue to extend our love and encouragement to all, hoping and praying for the success of families in time and/or eternity, while supporting one another in our seeming successes or failures. Satan makes a graven image of the perfect family to use as an implement of discouragement and failure.

Within traditional Christianity there have been many graven images formed of the Lord himself. They have been forged and fashioned over years of apostasy because of the confusion of gospel doctrine modified by men. Various images depict a god hard to identify in form, concept, or personal attributes. Though they carry the name of "Christ," they lack the attributes of the true God.

Often an accusation is made against the Latter-day Saints for failing to conform with "traditional" Christianity; hence, they say, the Mormons are not Christians. It is true that Latter-day Saints do not revere the graven images of modified Christianity. Consistent with the ancients, members of The Church of Jesus Christ of Latter-day Saints hold to the original truths revealed and reconfirmed by direct revelation from Christ to His living prophets. There is no need for graven images that approximate the true and living God, and no need to apologize for the rejection of graven images in favor of the God being imitated. As Elder Brockbank said, "The belief that God has no body, parts, and passions is not a doctrine of Jesus Christ or a doctrine of the holy scriptures but is a doctrine of men, and to worship such a God is in vain."[8]

What may threaten in the Church usually rules in the world. The symbols of violence, sex, wealth, and power freely hang as graven images in the dens and palaces of modern-day Gadianton robbers. Is it any surprise that both the supplier and the broker of all these graven images is Satan? As in premortal life, he still offers the wares of trickery and deceit, dripping in the overlay of imitation gold.

Where, then, is safety in a world of graven images? Ironically, it is found in an image: the image of God. When men stop engraving worldly images and allow themselves to be engraven upon with godly attributes (the image of Christ—see Alma 5:14), then they are "born again" and become Latter-day Saints. The image of God comes from above through the atoning blessings of Christ. When monuments and memorials, symbols and signs, and the activities and possessions of mankind are used to point others towards Christ, then there will be no condemnation. Beauty, peace, and progress will result. When men promote anything that leads away from godly attributes, then comes the violation of the second commandment: "Thou shalt not make unto thee any graven image" (Exodus 20:4).

There is a great truth often unperceived within the first and second commandments. When Jehovah said "Thou shalt have no other gods before me; thou shalt not make unto thee any graven image" (Exodus 20:3–4), He was not only giving a commandment but was also stating a truth as solid and final as eternity itself. When the doors of mortality open to the immortal realm, there is only one way to the degrees of glory: Christ. As Peter testified, "Neither is there salvation in any other: for there is none other name under heaven given among men, whereby we must be saved" (Acts 4:12).

Even those who worship and serve false gods and images (Satan included as a false god), and who pay penalties in hell, must some time come forth from the prison doors and turn to the one true God who holds the keys of death, hell, salvation, and exaltation: Jesus, the Christ. The Savior (not false gods and graven images) "saves all the works of his hands, except those sons of perdition who deny the Son after the Father has revealed him" (D&C 76:43). There are three degrees of glory, and all must come in mortality or immortality to the one true God in order to enter. And they must accept Him as their Savior of their own free will.

President Kimball bore witness that

the time will come when there will be a surrender of every person who has ever lived on this earth, who is now living, or who ever will live on this earth; and it will be an unforced surrender, an unconditional surrender. When will it be for you? Today? In twenty years? Two hundred years? Two thousand or a million? When? Again . . . I say, it is not *if* you will capitulate to the great truth; it is *when,* for I know that you cannot indefinitely resist the power and pressure of truth. Why not now?[9]

Therefore, in the end, we will have no other gods before Him, for there are none. We will not make unto us any graven images, for such will be useless as regards getting us into a degree of glory. What is a commandment in mortality is a fact in eternity! We worship a kind, loving, and forgiving God; a personal Savior leading us by the Spirit of Truth to the Father in whose image we were created. That is the only true image we seek as faithful Latter-day Saints.

Notes

1. *Hymns,* 1985, 301.

2. Marion G. Romney, in Conference Report, October 1978, 18.

3. Russell M. Nelson, *The Power Within Us* (Salt Lake City: Deseret Book, 1988), 125.

4. Brigham Young, in *Journal of Discourses,* 8:159–60.

5. Bernard P. Brockbank, in Conference Report, April 1977, 38.

6. Spencer W. Kimball, "The False Gods We Worship," *Ensign,* June 1976, 4.

7. Ibid.

8. Bernard P. Brockbank, *Ensign,* May 1977, 27.

9. Spencer W. Kimball, "Absolute Truth," *Ensign,* September 1978, 8.

3

"Thou Shalt Not Take the Name of the Lord Thy God In Vain"

DAVID ROLPH SEELY

THE LORD GAVE THE TEN Commandments on Mount Sinai to the children of Israel, who received them by covenant (see Exodus 20, 24). These commandments were written by the finger of the Lord on stone tablets (see Exodus 31:18), which were to be kept in the ark of the covenant (Deuteronomy 10:5), and were written in the book of the law which is found in the Old Testament. They represented for Israel the totality of the covenant. In early Jewish traditions they were recited each day in the temple, following the sacrifices.[1] Abinadi read them in his condemnation of the priests of Noah, and each is found throughout the Book of Mormon.[2] Their importance was reiterated by the Savior in the Sermon on the Mount (Matthew 5–7) and

David Rolph Seely is a member of the faculty of Ancient Scripture at Brigham Young University. He coauthored My Father's House: Temple Worship and Symbolism in the New Testament. *He and his wife, Jo Ann, are the parents of four children.*

throughout His ministry. Today each of the commandments is also part of the new and everlasting covenant and is found in the book of Doctrine and Covenants as part of the law of the Church in the latter days. These commandments are simple and yet profound statements of our relationship to our Father in Heaven and our relationship with each other as His children.

The Ten Commandments divide naturally into two parts. The first four commandments acknowledge the sovereignty of the Lord God of Israel and instruct covenant Israel regarding the proper respect and worship of Him. There is a logical progression to the ordering of these commandments. First, Israel is to put no other god before Him; second, they are not to make any graven image; third, they are not to use His name in vain; and fourth, they are to worship Him on the Sabbath day. These commandments form the basis for the next six commandments, which legislate the proper relationship between His children: to honor parents, and to avoid murder, adultery, stealing, false witness, and coveting.

The third commandment deals with the proper regard and usage of the name of God—a commandment which has far-reaching implications for Latter-day Saints in terms of both their communication and their behavior. The Lord has identified this commandment as an important one for us in the latter days, "Wherefore, let all men beware how they take my name in their lips" (D&C 63:61). When the Saints were preparing to leave Winter Quarters for the Salt Lake Valley in the winter of 1847 the Lord said to them, "Keep yourselves from evil to take the name of the Lord in vain, for I am the Lord your God, even the God of your fathers, the God of Abraham and of Isaac and of Jacob" (D&C 136:21).

"THOU SHALT NOT TAKE THE NAME OF THE LORD THY GOD IN VAIN"

A review of the meaning of each part of the third commandment reveals many important details that we often overlook. For example, what is meant by the phrase "thou shalt" or "thou shalt not"? What is the name of the Lord? What are the proper ways of taking the name of the Lord? And what does it mean to take His name "in vain"?

"Thou Shalt Not"

Most of the Ten Commandments begin with "thou shalt" or "thou shalt not." These phrases are the singular form of the command addressed to each member of the covenant rather than the group as a whole. Whereas often we envisage the law of Moses as given to all of Israel together, it is important to remember that each person entered into the covenant individually, and to remember the commitment each individual makes as he or she enters the covenant to keep each of the commandments. The Ten Commandments are not just commandments given to the Church but are to be taken as personal obligations for each member of the Church.

All but two of the commandments—honoring parents and keeping the Sabbath day holy—are phrased in the negative, "Thou shalt not." On a surface level negative commandments provide for us straightforward standards by which to direct our lives—don't have any other gods before the Lord, don't worship idols, don't take the Lord's name in vain; don't kill, commit adultery, steal, lie, and covet. At a deeper level, however, negative commandments invite us to reflect on what is meant and to consider what it is the Lord would have us do. In the Sermon on the Mount the Savior used two of the negative commandments to teach us the proper approach to all of the commandments. For example, He taught us that it is not enough not to kill or not to commit adultery. The proper understanding of these commandments, respectively, includes not getting angry and not lusting in our hearts (Matthew 5:21–32). In other words, the Ten Commandments emphasize on the surface proper *behavior* and yet at a deeper level are meant to demonstrate to us not just what we should do or not do but also what manner of people we should be on the *inside*. This is the case of the third commandment: we should first strive to refrain from taking the Lord's name in vain, and then we should ask ourselves how we should properly use His name in our lives.

"The Name of the Lord"

In the third commandment we find a very important phrase—"take the name of the Lord." First let us examine what is meant by the "name of the Lord." God has many names in the Old Testament and all of them are sacred. First and foremost is the name represented in Hebrew by the tetragrammaton *YHWH,* which in English is rendered as *Jehovah.* This was the most common name of God in ancient Israel and hence the most frequently used in the Old Testament text. It occurs over 6800 times in the Old Testament. It is the name by which Jesus Christ was known in the Old Testament—and was used by ancient Israel both publicly and privately in covenant-making, in prayer, and in blessing and praising God.

Through time, probably sometime in the first century before Christ, the third commandment was interpreted very strictly within Jewish tradition, and the name of God—which in Old Testament times was used in public and private worship—was considered so sacred that it was not allowed to be uttered except by the high priest on the Day of Atonement.[3] With the destruction of the temple in A.D. 70 the pronunciation of this sacred name was lost, since the Hebrew text of the Old Testament did not yet contain vowels. When the Massoretes put the vowels in the Hebrew text of the Bible beginning in the sixth century A.D. they put the vowels of the Hebrew word for *Lord* (Hebrew *Adonai*) with the four consonants of the sacred name (*YHWH*). Thus whenever a Jew in reading the Bible came to the name *YHWH* (Jehovah) he or she would simply say "Adonai" rather than attempt to pronounce the name. The King James translators respected this tradition and, with just a few exceptions,[4] when they came to the word *YHWH* in the Hebrew text they rendered it in English as LORD, with small capital letters, to protect the sanctity of the name.

This demonstration of respect for the holy name of God is very similar to the Lord's authorizing His people to call *the Holy Priesthood, after the Order of the Son of God* the Melchizedek Priesthood "out of respect or reverence to the name of the Supreme Being, to avoid the too frequent repetition of his name" (D&C 107:2–4). So while the King James Version of the Bible only rarely uses the name *Jehovah,* we must remember that the frequently occurring English word *LORD* is the word that represents His name (*YHWH*) in the text and we should use it with reverence.

The other most common name for Deity in the scriptures is *God,* which is the English translation of Hebrew *Elohim* (in Hebrew a plural form meaning "gods"). Thus the word *God* is also a sacred name or title of Deity and should be used with the utmost respect.

From the premortal life Jehovah, Jesus Christ, was also known as the Only Begotten of the Father or simply as the Son. The Lord revealed to Moses, "the name of [the] Only Begotten is the Son of Man, even Jesus Christ" (Moses 6:57). When Jehovah was born into mortality the Lord instructed His parents to name Him Jesus (see Matthew 1:21; Luke 1:31). Because He is the Messiah, or Anointed One, He is called Jesus Christ—*Christ* being the Greek word meaning "anointed one." These are the names and titles by which we have been instructed to enter covenants, offer prayer, and perform priesthood ordinances—in the name of the Son, or Jesus Christ. Thus, the third commandment applies to the usage of all the names and titles of Deity.

"Thou Shalt Not Take the Name of the Lord Thy God"

Ancient Israel was commanded "Thou shalt fear the Lord thy God, and serve him, and shalt swear by his name" (Deuteronomy 6:13). Let us review here some of the proper ways to "take the name of the Lord."

We must remember that the biblical society was administered under the law of Moses and there was not a division between church and state, as many of us are accustomed to in modern times. Thus under the law of Moses legal oaths and covenants were also entered into with the name of the Lord. Testimony was given in court and sworn in the name of God. The complete form of biblical oaths included a self-curse ensuring that the one swearing the oath was telling the truth. See, for example, the incident where Saul forbade anyone to eat. Upon catching his son Jonathan who had inadvertently broken his father's vow, Saul answered, "God do so and more also [assuming some self-curse]5: for thou shalt surely die, Jonathan" (1 Samuel 14:44; see also Ruth 1:17; 1 Samuel 3:17; 2 Samuel 3:35; and 1 Kings 2:23). This is one form of taking an oath in the name of the Lord. Elsewhere God is called to witness the covenant (see Genesis 31:50; 1 Samuel 12:5; 20:23) and a common oath-making phrase is "as the Lord liveth" (Judges 8:19; 1 Samuel 14:39, 45; 19:6; 20:3, 21).6

Under the law of Moses the name of God was very important and was used by covenant people both in taking upon themselves religious covenants or obligations, which were administrated and sworn to by the name of God, and in legal situations where a testimony was given and affirmed by a solemn oath in the name of Deity. Both of these usages of the name of Deity were considered to be legitimate and were so serious that to take such an oath in the name of God and then not to live up to that oath, or to make a testimony in court falsely using the name of God, was a capital offense. Isaiah was referring to such oath- and covenant-making when he said, "Hear ye this, O house of Jacob, which are called by the name of Israel, and are come forth out of the waters of Judah [or out of the waters of baptism—1 Nephi 20:1], which swear by the name of the Lord, and make mention of the God of Israel, but not in truth, nor in righteousness" (Isaiah 48:1).

"In Vain"

The phrase "in vain" is a translation of the Hebrew prepositional phrase *lashaw*, which means "worthless" or "without result." It is the same phrase found in Psalm 24:3–4, which defines who is worthy to stand in the presence of the Lord at the temple: "Who shall ascend into the hill of the Lord? or who shall stand in his holy place? He that hath clean hands, and a pure heart; who hath not lifted up his soul *unto vanity,* nor sworn deceitfully." This phrase is also used in Jeremiah 2:30, where the Lord says, "In vain have I smitten your children; they received no correction." The word *vain* is also often found in the context of hypocrisy. In Isaiah 1:13 the Lord admonished Israel that they were to "Bring no more vain oblations" to the temple until they had repented first of their wickedness.

The Hebrew term *vain* can be used to mean "falsely" as well. The ninth commandment in Deuteronomy 5:20, "Neither shalt thou bear *false* witness against thy neighbor," uses the same Hebrew word translated as "vain" in the third commandment in Exodus 20:7. An additional reference to the third commandment in the Old Testament replaces the word *vain* with the Hebrew term meaning "falsely." Leviticus 19:12 expands on the third commandment: "And ye shall not swear by my name falsely, neither shalt thou profane the name of thy God: I am the Lord." In this passage the Hebrew word *leshaqer* is used, which means "falsely" (see also Leviticus 6:3). The third commandment should be understood as condemning taking the name of the Lord "in vain" which has several related meanings. We are not to take His name lightly, or without effect, with no intention of fulfilling our promise. We should not take His name hypocritically—outwardly showing piety when we are not repentant. And we should not take His name "falsely," deliberately attempting to deceive others into thinking we are earnest in our commitments to the Lord when we are not.

"FOR THE LORD WILL NOT HOLD HIM GUILTLESS THAT TAKETH HIS NAME IN VAIN"

In both the Mosaic Law and the higher law the Lord often spells out the specific blessings for obeying the covenant and the specific curses for disobedience. The blessings and curses of the

Mosaic covenant are found in Deuteronomy 27–29 promising the covenant people prosperity, peace, and protection for their obedience and famine, war, and destruction for their disobedience. This commandment about taking the name of the Lord in vain also contains a stern reminder of the serious nature of this sin—that the Lord will not hold the offenders guiltless (see Exodus 20:7).

The Old Testament contains a specific story that illustrates the breaking of each of nine of the Ten Commandments and stands as a witness to the people of the serious nature of these commandments.[7] All of these episodes add up to a systematic breaking of the covenant Israel made at Sinai as recorded in the books of Genesis through 2 Kings. The Lord in turn invoked the punishments decreed in Deuteronomy 27–29 and punished the people by eventual destruction and exile recounted in 2 Kings 25. The breaking of the first two commandments is found in the story of the golden calf in Exodus 32, where the people sought after another god and crafted an image of him that they attempted to worship. The breaking of the third commandment is found in a short story in Leviticus 24:10–16. It is recorded that a certain "son of an Israelitish woman, whose father was an Egyptian, went out among the children of Israel: and this son of the Israelitish woman and a man of Israel strove together in the camp; and the Israelitish woman's son blasphemed the name of the Lord, and cursed" (Leviticus 24:10–11). The man was taken before Moses for judgment and Moses inquired of the Lord. The Lord emphasized the serious nature of this offense when He said, "Bring forth him that hath cursed without the camp; and let all that heard him lay their hands upon his head, and let all the congregation stone him" (Leviticus 24:14). The passage records that the children of Israel fulfilled the Lord's commandment and stoned the man to death. Under the law of Moses blaspheming the name of the Lord—in this case to take His sacred name in a curse—was a capital offense just as were murder and adultery. The Lord has not pronounced the same punishment in the latter days, but the serious nature of blasphemy makes it a grievous sin.

"WHEREFORE, LET ALL MEN BEWARE HOW THEY TAKE MY NAME IN THEIR LIPS—" D&C 63:61

In the latter days the Lord has given us a solemn warning about how we take His name on our lips (see D&C 63:61). This commandment, which protects the sanctity of the name of God, is a far-reaching commandment that applies to many different aspects of our speech. From the scriptures written by ancient prophets and the teachings of modern prophets let us review the proper usage of the name of the Lord. From these inspired teachings we will examine five specific applications of this commandment: prayer, repentance, ordinances and covenants, proper authority, blasphemy and profanity.

Prayer

After Adam and Eve were cast out of the Garden, they offered sacrifices to God as He had commanded. Through an angel the Lord sent to them it was explained that these sacrifices were in the similitude of the sacrifice of the Only Begotten of the Father. The angel further commanded them, "Wherefore, thou shalt do all that thou doest in the name of the Son, and thou shalt repent and call upon God in the name of the Son forevermore" (Moses 5:8). One of the most frequent occasions in which we take the name of the Lord is in prayer. In the Sermon on the Mount Jesus taught us how to pray both by instruction and by example. He especially cautioned us against hypocrisy: "And when thou prayest, thou shalt not be as the hypocrites are: for they love to pray standing in the synagogues and in the corners of the streets, that they may be seen of men" (Matthew 6:5). In addition He warned us against "vain repetitions": "But when ye pray, use not vain repetitions, as the heathen do: for they think that they shall be heard for their much speaking" (Matthew 6:7). (We should notice that it is not the repetitions that are condemned but rather the "*vain* repetitions.") Then He gave us an example of prayer illustrating the proper regard for calling upon the name of God: "Our Father which art in heaven, Hallowed be thy name" (Matthew 6:9).

One of the most important scriptural passages about prayer is found in Amulek's sermon to the Zoramites. He taught that they must exercise their faith unto repentance by calling upon the holy name of God, that they should humble themselves, that they should continually pray in their fields and their households for their own welfare and the welfare of others. Most important, He closes His sermon as follows: "And now behold, my beloved brethren, I say unto you, do not suppose that this is all; for after ye have done all these things, if ye turn away the needy, and the naked, and visit not the sick and afflicted, and impart of your substance, if ye have, to those who stand in need—I say unto you, if ye do not any of these things, behold, your prayer is vain, and availeth you nothing, and ye are as hypocrites who do deny the faith" (Alma 34:28).

If we take the name of the Lord in prayer to be "seen of men," in "vain repetitions," or in praying for the welfare of others without charity and the willingness to help, we have "taken his name in vain."

Repentance

Likewise the admonition to Adam and Eve included the use of the name of God in the process of repentance: "Wherefore, thou shalt do all that thou doest in the name of the Son, and thou shalt repent and call upon God in the name of the Son forevermore" (Moses 5:8).

Repentance that brings forgiveness is possible only through the atonement of Jesus Christ and must be done through His name. All men and women have been invited to come to Him and partake of His atonement, but in order to do so they must confess Him and repent in His name. In the Book of Mormon we have a dramatic illustration of this process. King Benjamin gathered his people together and taught them about the Atonement.

The people were overcome by the Spirit and fell to the earth, repenting of their sins, "O have mercy, and apply the atoning blood of Christ that we may receive forgiveness of our sins, and our hearts may be purified; for we believe in Jesus Christ, the Son of God" (Mosiah 4:2). The people received a remission of their sins and entered into a covenant with the Lord. King Benjamin responded to their conversion: "And now, because of the covenant which ye have made ye shall be called the children of Christ, his sons, and his daughters; for behold, this day he hath spiritually begotten you; for ye say that your hearts are changed through faith on his name; therefore, ye are born of him and have become his sons and his daughters" (Mosiah 5:7). King Benjamin then recorded the names of the people "who had entered into a covenant with God to keep his commandments" (Mosiah 6:1).

Thus a proper way of taking the name of the Lord is in humility to repent of our sins in the name of the Only Begotten, Jesus Christ. To attempt to repent without humility or acknowledgment of His atonement is an example of taking the name of the Lord in vain. To attempt to cover our sins or pretend to repent when we are not repentant is an example of taking His name falsely.

Ordinances and Covenants

As we have noted above, the Lord commanded Israel, under the law of Moses, "Thou shalt fear the Lord thy God, and serve him, and shalt swear by his name" (Deuteronomy 6:13). The same principle is taught in the Book of Mormon: "There shall be no other name given nor any other way nor means whereby salvation can come unto the children of men, only in and through the name of Christ, the Lord Omnipotent" (Mosiah 3:17). And in the New Testament: "Neither is there salvation in any other: for there is none other name under heaven given among men, whereby we must be saved" (Acts 4:12).

All of the ordinances of salvation, including repentance and prayer, baptism, and the bestowal of the gift of the Holy Ghost, are to be done in the name of Deity. Baptisms are to be performed specifically "in the name of the Father, and of the Son, and of the Holy Ghost." A proper way of taking the name of God upon us is to enter into these ordinances with humility, with honesty, and with full intent to fulfill our obligations. Those seeking baptism are to take upon themselves through that ordinance the name of Christ (D&C 20:37), the only name under heaven through which we can be saved. Partakers of the sacrament specifically renew this covenant when they witness that they are willing to take upon them the name of the Son, that they will remember Him, and that they will keep His commandments (see D&C 20:77–79). The Lord has promised that "signs shall follow them that believe" through the name of Jesus Christ, including the healing of the sick and the casting out of devils (see D&C 35:9; 84:66–72).

Willful rebellion against these covenants and the refusal or neglect to fulfill our obligations are prime examples of "taking his name in vain." In the latter days the Lord has warned the members of the Church, "Behold, I, the Lord, have looked upon you, and have seen abominations in the church that profess my name" (D&C 50:4); "ye that hear me not will I curse, that have professed my name, with the heaviest of all cursings" (D&C 41:1). The Lord has defined this kind of behavior as blasphemy of His name and has warned that the judgments of God will begin with His own house: "And upon my house shall it begin, and from my house shall it go forth, saith the Lord; first among those among you, saith the Lord, who have professed to know my name and have not known me, and have blasphemed against me in the midst of my house" (D&C 112:25–26).

As we have discussed above, many of the oaths and covenants under the Law of Moses were entered into with the name of the Lord. The commandment in Leviticus about swearing "falsely" is related to this. Apparently, at the time of Jesus solemn formulas of oath-taking were commonly used in mundane situations where one making a promise would swear by the heavens, or by Jerusalem, in place of God, thus dramatizing his or her intention to fulfill the promise. Jesus responded to such "forswearing" when He taught in the Sermon on the Mount: "Swear not at all; neither by heaven; for it is God's throne: nor by the earth; for it is his footstool: . . . But let your communication be, Yea, yea; Nay, nay: for whatsoever is more than these cometh of evil" (Matthew 5:34–35, 37). Jesus was teaching the importance of honesty in all of our dealings with our fellowmen, and that sacred oath formulas should be reserved for sacred covenant-making and not used for the mundane.

Such oaths of frivolous forswearing can also be found in modern language. For example, remnants of the self-curses can be found on the playground where children often say such things as "Cross my heart, hope to die, stick a needle in my eye." Likewise, much profanity in our culture is a frivolous usage of what once were sacred oaths. When people say, "By such and such," or "I'll be ———" we can see vestiges of ancient biblical solemn-oath formulas.

There are many occasions in which we make oaths in American culture. We sign our names as a guarantee when we write a check, borrow money, marry, or sign our tax returns. In legal situations, swearing to tell the truth in court used to always entail putting one's hand on a Bible and invoking God, reciting, "I swear to tell the truth, the whole truth, and nothing but the truth—so help me God." Today this has been substituted in many situations with a simple oath of affirmation. Nevertheless, in Jesus' sermon about the seriousness of forswearing, all of these situations, whether we invoke the name of God or not, call for absolute honesty.

Authority

The Lord has made it clear from the beginning that all priesthood ordinances are to be done in the name of Deity and must be done by those who have the proper authority and, where appropriate, keys: "Wherefore, let all men beware how they take my name in their lips—for behold, verily I say, that many there be who are under this condemnation, who use the name of the Lord, and use it in vain, having not authority" (D&C 63:61–62).

President Spencer W. Kimball taught: "Presumptuous and blasphemous are they who purport to baptize, bless, marry, or perform other sacraments in the name of the Lord while in fact lacking his specific authorization. And no one can obtain God's authority from reading the Bible or from just a desire to serve the Lord, no matter how pure his motives."[8] Those who attempt to work in His name without proper authority "take the name of the Lord in vain" and break the third commandment.

Blasphemy and Profanity

Jesus taught: "Not that which goeth into the mouth defileth a man; but that which cometh out of the mouth, this defileth a man" (Matthew 15:11). The Epistle of James further teaches that control of one's tongue represents self-mastery as a whole, and he warns us of the possible effects of unbridled speech:

> Even so the tongue is a little member, and boasteth great things. Behold, how great a matter a little fire kindleth!
>
> And the tongue is a fire, a world of iniquity: so is the tongue among our members, that it defileth the whole body, and setteth on fire the course of nature; and it is set on fire of hell.
>
> For every kind of beasts, and of birds, and of serpents, and of things in the sea, is tamed, and hath been tamed of mankind:
>
> But the tongue can no man tame; it is an unruly evil, full of deadly poison.
>
> Therewith bless we God, even the Father; and therewith curse we men, which are made after the similitude of God.
>
> Out of the same mouth proceedeth blessing and cursing. My brethren, these things ought not so to be.
>
> Doth a fountain send forth at the same place sweet water and bitter? (James 3:5–11.)

For the better or the worse our verbal expressions reveal much about what we are like inside. Control of our speech reflects the control that we have over many aspects of our lives. So while the third commandment specifically commands us not to use the name of the Lord in vain—in prayer, oath taking and covenant-making, and without authority—the scriptures and modern prophets and Apostles have taught that the third commandment extends to any irreverent use of the name of God and by extension to unclean and impure language of any kind. The *Encyclopedia of Mormonism* comments: "General Authorities of the Church have defined profanity to include the following: (1) blasphemy (irreverent use of the Lord's name); (2) swearing; (3) vulgarity (coarse jokes, foul stories, lewd words); (4) use of the Lord's name without proper authority; and (5) any type of filthiness in speech that is degrading and soul-destroying."9

Many of the modern prophets have given us counsel about the rise of profanity and unclean speech in our society, in the media, even among the Saints. President Kimball gave several memorable addresses about this commandment. Many of us remember the numerous surgeries he had for his health through the years. He once recounted a personal experience he had in one of his many stays at the hospital:

"In the hospital one day I was wheeled out of the operating room by an attendant who stumbled, and there issued from his angry lips vicious cursing with a combination of the names of the Savior. Even half-conscious, I recoiled and implored: 'Please! Please! That is my Lord whose names you revile.'

"There was a deathly silence, then a subdued voice whispered, 'I am sorry.' He had forgotten for the moment that the Lord had forcefully commanded all his people, 'Thou shalt not take the name of the Lord thy God in vain' (Exodus 20:7.)"10 President Kimball went on to relate that such language demonstrates many things about a person: that they do not have self-control, and that they do not demonstrate gratitude towards God. One of President Kimball's most notable observations about unclean speech was, "Profanity is the effort of a feeble brain to express itself forcibly."11

In a conference talk in 1987 when he was First Counselor in the First Presidency, President Gordon B. Hinckley reported that in our society such profanity is becoming all too prevalent. He read from a First Presidency general epistle issued a hundred years earlier, dated 8 April 1887 which stated: "The habit . . . , which some young people fall into of using vulgarity and profanity . . . is not only offensive to well-bred persons, but it is a gross sin in the sight of God, and should not exist among the children of Latter-day Saints."[12] In addition President Hinckley recounted the story of the son of the Israelitish woman who was stoned to death for blasphemy (see Leviticus 16) and said "While that most serious of penalties has long since ceased to be inflicted, the gravity of the sin has not changed."[13]

The third commandment focuses attention on the importance of honoring and respecting the name of the Lord. It is a commandment that covers many aspects of our lives—how we think of God, how we address Him, how we refer to Him, and our integrity in honoring the covenants we have made with Him. It reminds us of the need to do everything in His name—for the reverence with which we utter His name is a reflection of our inner commitment to Him. The High Priest in ancient Israel, when he officiated in the tabernacle and later the temple, wore a plate of pure gold on his forehead inscribed "Holiness to the Lord" meaning that the priest was dedicated and consecrated to the Lord (see Exodus 39:30). It was a graphic symbol that he had taken the name of the Lord—Jehovah—upon himself and was striving to be worthy of bearing that name. In this he represented all of Israel, who were called to be "a kingdom of priests, and an holy nation" (Exodus 19:6).

In a less dramatic fashion I remember the feeling I had when I first became a missionary wearing my name tag bearing the name of The Church of Jesus Christ of Latter-day Saints and the great responsibility I felt in wearing His name on my jacket pocket. Members of the Church through the waters of baptism have taken His name upon themselves in a sacred covenant. To those who are faithful in taking upon themselves the name of the

Son in mortality the Lord has promised that they can come forth with Him on Mount Zion at the Second Coming, with the name of the Father written on their foreheads (see Revelation 14:1; D&C 133:18). For it is only through the name of the Son that we can have the fulness of the Father.

Notes

1. Mishnah, *Tamid* 5.1.

2. See David Rolph Seely, "The Ten Commandments in the Book of Mormon," pp. 166–81 in *Doctrines of the Book of Mormon, The 1991 Sperry Symposium,* ed. Bruce A. Van Orden and Brent L. Top (Salt Lake City: Deseret Book, 1992).

3. According to the Mishnah, *Yoma* 3:8 on the Day of Atonement the high priest recited the prayer in Leviticus 16:30, "For on this day shall atonement be made for you to cleanse you; from all your sins shall ye be clean before the Lord"—at which point he actually pronounced before the people the name of the Lord *YHWH*. See *The Mishnah,* translated by Herbert Danby (Oxford: Oxford University Press), 165 note no. 8.

4. The word *Jehovah* is retained in the KJV in Exodus 6:3; Psalm 83:18; Isaiah 12:2; 26:4 and in several titles such as Jehovah-jireh (Genesis 22:14); Jehovah-nissi (Exodus 17:15); Jehovah-shalom (Judges 6:24).

5. One example of a self-curse in biblical oath-making is found in Jeremiah 34 where the people entering into a covenant "cut the calf in twain, and passed between the parts thereof" (Jeremiah 34:18) apparently as a sign that they too would be cut in two if they did not fulfill their obligation.

6. For a good discussion of biblical oaths see M.H. Pope, "Oaths," *Interpreter's Dictionary of the Bible,* ed. G. A. Buttrick et al. (Nashville and New York: Abingdon Press, 1962), 3:575–77.

7. See David Noel Freedman, "The Nine Commandments: The Secret Progress of Israel's Sins," *Bible Review V,* no. 6 (December 1989), 28–37, 42. The breaking of the first two commandments is found in the incident of the golden calf in Exodus 32. The breaking of the third commandment is found in a short story in Leviticus 24:10–16 where a man blasphemed the name of God. The breaking of the Sabbath is found in Numbers 15:32–36, dishonoring of parents in Deuteronomy 21:18–21; murder in Judges 9, adultery in 2 Samuel 11–12, stealing in Joshua 7, and bearing false witness in 1 Kings 21. While there is no single story that is solely about coveting, it plays a major role in the stories of David and Bathsheba (2 Samuel 11–12), and Ahab, Jezebel, and Naboth (1 Kings 21).

8. Spencer W. Kimball, *The Miracle of Forgiveness* (Salt Lake City: Bookcraft, 1969), 55.

9. *Encyclopedia of Mormonism*, s.v. "Profanity," 3:1158.

10. Spencer W. Kimball, "President Kimball Speaks Out on Profanity," *Ensign*, February 1981, 3.

11. Spencer W. Kimball, "God Will Not Be Mocked," *Ensign*, November 1974, 7.

12. *Messages of the First Presidency*, comp. James R. Clark, 6 vols. (Salt Lake City: Bookcraft, 1965–75), 3:112–13.

13. Gordon B. Hinckley, "Take Not the Name of God in Vain," *Ensign*, November 1987, 45–46.

4

"Remember the Sabbath Day, to Keep It Holy"

ROBERT L. MILLET

*J*EHOVAH COMMANDED: "Remember the sabbath day, to keep it holy. Six days shalt thou labour, and do all thy work; but the seventh day is the sabbath of the Lord thy God: in it thou shalt not do any work, thou, nor thy son, nor thy daughter, thy manservant, nor thy maidservant, nor thy cattle, nor thy stranger that is within thy gates: for in six days the Lord made heaven and earth, the sea, and all that in them is, and rested the seventh day: wherefore the Lord blessed the sabbath day, and hallowed it." (Exodus 20:8–11.)

BACKGROUNDS

The observance of the Sabbath predates Sinai, for we learn

***Robert L. Millet** is dean of Religious Education at Brigham Young University. He has authored or coauthored many books, including the* Doctrinal Commentary on the Book of Mormon *series. He and his wife, Shauna, are the parents of six children.*

from Moses that after the Gods had completed the paradisiacal creation of all things, the Lord "rested on the seventh day from all his work which he had made. And God blessed the seventh day, and sanctified it: because that in it he had rested from all his work which God created and made." (Genesis 2:2–3; see also Moses 3:2–3.)

Interestingly, there is no mention in the Old Testament about the Sabbath or Sabbath observance during the times of Abraham, Isaac, and Jacob, but we would suppose, knowing the import of this statute, that the Former-day Saints during patriarchal times did in fact honor the seventh day as a holy memorial. From the time of the Exodus of the children of Israel from Egypt, the Sabbath commemorated the deliverance of the covenant people from bondage. "Keep the sabbath day to sanctify it, as the Lord thy God hath commanded thee. . . . And remember that thou wast a servant in the land of Egypt, and that the Lord thy God brought thee out thence through a mighty hand and by a stretched out arm: therefore the Lord thy God commanded thee to keep the sabbath day." (Deuteronomy 5:12, 15.) This would mean, therefore, that the Sabbath that commemorated the Exodus was kept on a different day each year.

During the wilderness wanderings the Israelites were instructed to gather enough manna on the day prior to the Sabbath so that they would have sufficient. "And Moses said, Eat that to day: for to day is a sabbath unto the Lord: to day ye shall not find it in the field. Six days ye shall gather it; but on the seventh day, which is the sabbath, in it there shall be none." (Exodus 16:25–26.) Indeed, the seriousness of the law of the Sabbath is illustrated in an instance recorded in Numbers 15, in which "a man that gathered sticks upon the sabbath day" was stoned to death by the congregation of Israel (vv. 32–36).

Inasmuch as a proper observance of the Sabbath signals and symbolizes a worshipful attitude, it would seem to follow that during periods of waywardness the people of God would naturally cease to comply with this law. Thus Nehemiah's reform included a reinstitution of a strict Sabbath observance. "In those days saw I in Judah some treading wine presses on the sabbath, and bringing in sheaves, and lading asses. . . . Then I contended with the nobles of Judah, and said unto them, What evil thing is this that ye do, and profane the sabbath day? Did not your fathers thus, and did not our God bring all this evil upon us, and upon this city? yet ye bring more wrath upon Israel by profaning the sabbath. And it came to pass, that when the gates of Jerusalem began to be dark before the sabbath, I commanded that the gates should be shut, and charged that they should not be opened till after the sabbath: and some of my servants set I at the gates, that there should no burden be brought in on the sabbath day." (Nehemiah 13:15–19.)

During the centuries preceding the coming of the Messiah, efforts to interpret the law resulted in massive commentary, rules, and "traditions of the elders." No aspect of the law became more burdensome and cumbersome than the law of the Sabbath. Endless lists and formulae pertaining to servile work, distances to be travelled, and in general what was and was not appropriate for the Sabbath—these things constituted an integral part of daily life among Jews in the first century. "We do not overstate our case," Elder Bruce R. McConkie has written, "when we say that the Jewish system of Sabbath observance that prevailed in the day of Jesus was ritualistic, degenerate, and almost unbelievably absurd, a system filled with fanatical restrictions."[1] In an effort to establish a sane perspective on the Sabbath day—to point up the spiritual inconsistency associated with so many inane restrictions— Jesus took occasion to lift and teach and heal and work miracles, to do good, on the Sabbath, for all of which He was attacked by His enemies among the Jewish leaders. "Wherefore the Sabbath was given unto man for a day of rest," He taught; "and also that man should glorify God, and not that man should not eat; for the Son of Man made the Sabbath day, therefore the Son of Man is Lord also of the Sabbath" (JST, Mark 2:26–27). Following Jesus' mortal ministry, the members of The Church of Jesus Christ observed the first day of the week as the Sabbath day, the Lord's day, in remembrance of the resurrection of the Master (see Acts 20:7; 1 Corinthians 16:2; Revelation 1:10).

PURPOSES OF THE SABBATH

Why would God stress so forcefully the proper observance of the Sabbath? Why would this be one of the Ten Commandments? Consider the following principles:

1. *Acquiring Physical Rest.* In a very practical way, the Sabbath was given to man to enable us to take a break, to rest our tired bodies, to renew ourselves physically. So many in our modern age work themselves to exhaustion, work long days (and some even into the night), in an effort to get ahead financially and get a jump on rising costs. Too often they choose to work on the Sabbath, only to face themselves in the mirror on Monday mornings, unrested and unsatisfied. The body is the temple of God (see 1 Corinthians 3:16–17; 6:19), and we can do ourselves quite as much harm through overwork as we can by other more obvious forms of abuse.

2. *Acquiring Spiritual Rest.* Perhaps more important than our need for physical respite is our need for spiritual rest. Many of us face the world Monday through Saturday, face a hostile environment that tugs at our testimony and digs at our devotion. We engage a fallen world that too often weakens our resolve and entices us toward ungodliness. The Sabbath is fundamentally necessary in order to charge our batteries and empower our souls. President Brigham Young noted that "the Lord has planted within us a divinity; and that divine immortal spirit requires to be fed. Will earthly food answer for that purpose? No. It will only keep this body alive as long as the spirit stays with it." President Young also explained: "That divinity within us needs food from the Fountain from which it emanated."[2] "It is a day of worship," President Joseph F. Smith declared, "a day in which the spiritual life of man may be enriched. *A day of indolence, a day of physical recuperation is too often a very different thing from the God-ordained day of rest.* . . . A proper observance of the duties and devotions of the Sabbath day will, by its change and its spiritual life, give the best rest that men can enjoy on the Sabbath day."[3]

It is essential for us to go to church to participate in those sacraments or ordinances that provide a clear channel for divine power. "And that thou mayest more fully keep thyself unspotted from the world," Jehovah said in a modern revelation, "thou shalt go to the house of prayer and offer up thy sacraments upon my holy day; for verily this is a day appointed unto you to rest from your labors, and to pay thy devotions unto the Most High" (D&C 59:9–10). Partaking of the sacrament of the Lord's Supper enables us to renew sacred covenants—our promise to take the Lord's name, to keep His commandments, to bear one another's burdens—and to renew the Lord's promise to us—that we can be forgiven and renewed in spirit, that we may always have His Spirit to be with us (see Moroni 4–5).

There is a grander sense in which proper Sabbath observance rests our souls. Too many of us depend upon church attendance and weekly association with the Saints to make all the difference in our spiritual lives; we suppose that one-day-a-week holiness is sufficient for us to make it through the mists of darkness. I am persuaded that the Sabbath serves us most powerfully when we have earnestly sought through the week to come unto Christ— through at least brief, daily efforts at personal and family devotion. One of the reasons why we often have such difficulty pondering on the Savior and His atoning sacrifice during the sacramental service is that we have not thought much about such things Monday through Saturday. On the other hand, when members of the Church are striving to think and ponder and pray and search the scriptures during the week, then the Sabbath becomes a capstone to a well-spent week. It is of such seven-day-a-week holiness that the Master speaks when He says: "Nevertheless, thy vows shall be offered up in righteousness on all days and at all times" (D&C 59:11).

The scriptures often speak of *rest* in other ways as well. The Sabbath is a day of rest in the sense that it is a day wherein we seek to enter the "rest of the Lord," that is, "rest from doubt, from fear, from apprehension of danger, rest from the religious turmoil of the world."[4] To rest thus on the Sabbath is also to move closer to that supernal day when we are permitted to enter God's presence (see JST, Exodus 34:1–2) and receive the fulness of His glory (see D&C 84:24). We thus rest here, in this life, in preparation for the ultimate rest hereafter. Mormon declared: "Wherefore, I would speak unto you that are of the church, that are the peaceable followers of Christ, and that have obtained a sufficient hope by which ye can enter into the rest of the Lord, from this time henceforth until ye shall rest with him in heaven" (Moroni 7:3).

3. *Demonstrating Devotion to Deity.* As we have already suggested, the Sabbath allows us to focus, at least once per week, on matters of eternal import. We are all expected to cultivate the spirit of revelation and the spirit of Christian service every day of our lives, but the Sabbath provides us with a unique opportunity to divorce ourselves from the cares of Babylon—making money, meeting deadlines, competing—and give our full time and attention to the establishment of Zion. On the Sabbath we teach our families the gospel, study the scriptures and the words of the living oracles, and in general delight in the things of the Spirit. To observe the Sabbath, President Spencer W. Kimball wrote, "one will be on his knees in prayer, preparing lessons, studying the gospel, meditating, visiting the ill and distressed, sleeping, reading wholesome material, and attending all the meetings of that day to which he is expected."[5] President Harold B. Lee explained: "Sunday is more than a day of rest from the ordinary occupations of the week. It is not to be considered as merely a day of lazy indolence and idleness or for physical pleasures and indulgences. It is a feastday for your spirit bodies."[6]

Because the Lord established the Sabbath as a day of rest at the consummation of the Creation, it would be wise for us to reflect, on the Sabbath, on the goodness and omnipotence of our Creator, to ponder on the beauties and wonders about us. Because the Sabbath at one time in history commemorated the deliverance of ancient Israel from the hold of the Egyptians, it would be wise for us to reflect, on the Sabbath, on the power of the Almighty's arm to deliver us from ignorance and sin and death and eternal unhappiness. And because since the ministry of the Messiah the Sabbath has pointed us to His rise from death, it would be wise for us to reflect, on the Sabbath, on the infinite and eternal atoning sacrifice of Jesus the Christ. President David O. McKay observed: "Our Sabbath, the first day of the week, commemorates the greatest event in all history—Christ's resurrection, and his visit as a resurrected being to his assembled Apostles."[7] Elder Mark E. Petersen therefore added that "our observance or nonobservance of the Sabbath is an unerring measure of our attitude toward the Lord personally and toward his suffering in Gethsemane, his death on the cross, and his resurrection from the dead. It is a sign of whether we are Christians in very deed, or whether our conversion is so shallow that commemoration of his atoning sacrifice means little or nothing to us."[8]

PROPHETIC COUNSEL

The leaders of the Church have made it abundantly clear that God expects a covenant people to be true to their covenants, including our ongoing promise to properly observe the Sabbath. We cannot expect to avoid the perils that await the ungodly if we are contributors to society's ungodliness and irreverence. Elder George Albert Smith declared the following in a much quieter and more reverent day than our own: "The Sabbath has become the play-day of this great nation—the day set apart by thousands to violate the commandment that God gave long, long ago, and I am persuaded that much of the sorrow and distress that is afflicting and will continue to inflict mankind is traceable to the fact that they have ignored his admonition to keep the Sabbath day holy."[9] President Spencer W. Kimball stated: "I again would urge upon all Saints everywhere a more strict observance of the Sabbath day. The Lord's holy day is fast losing its sacred significance throughout the world, at least our world. More and more, man destroys the Sabbath's sacred purposes in pursuit of wealth, pleasure, recreation, and the worship of false and material gods."[10]

Also: "Brethren and sisters, once again I call to our attention the fourth commandment given by the Lord to Moses on Mount Sinai. . . . Let us observe it strictly in our homes and in our families. Let us refrain from all unnecessary labors. Sunday is not a day for hunting or fishing, nor for swimming, picnicking, boating, or engaging in any other sports."[11]

President Ezra Taft Benson stated: "I don't believe that it is possible to keep our spirituality on a high plane by spending our Sabbaths on the beach, on the golf course, in the mountains, or in our own homes reading newspapers and looking at television. When the Lord said, 'And that thou mayest more fully keep thyself unspotted from the world, thou shalt go to the house of prayer' (D&C 59:9), that is exactly what He meant. We must have spiritual food.

"Of course you can live a pretty good life out on the golf course on Sunday. But you don't build your spirituality. Probably you could worship the Lord out there, but the fact is you don't do it as you don't worship Him down on the beach. But if you go to the house of the Lord you will worship Him. If you attend to your prayers in your home with your family you will worship Him. And your spirituality will be raised. The spiritual food which your body requires will be provided and you will be much more apt to have this joy."[12]

Note the following counsel regarding purchases on the Sabbath:

"We note," President Kimball observed, "that in our Christian world in many places we still have business establishments open for business on the sacred Sabbath. We are sure the cure of this lies in ourselves, the buying public. Certainly the stores and business houses would not remain open if we, the people, failed to purchase from them. Will you all please reconsider this matter. Take it to your home evenings and discuss it with your children. It would be wonderful if every family determined that henceforth no Sabbath purchase would be made."[13]

"I wish I had the power," President Gordon B. Hinckley said, "to convert this whole Church to the observance of the Sabbath.

I know our people would be more richly blessed of the Lord if they would walk in faithfulness in the observance of the Sabbath. . . . There isn't anybody in this Church who has to buy furniture on Sunday. There really isn't. There isn't anybody in this Church who has to buy a new automobile on Sunday, is there? No. There isn't anybody in this Church who, with a little care and planning, has to buy groceries on Sunday. . . . You don't need to make Sunday a day of merchandising. . . . I don't think we need to patronize the ordinary business merchants on the Sabbath day. Why do they stay open? To get customers. Who are those customers? Well, they are not all nonmembers of this Church. You know that and I know that."[14]

Note the counsel from President James E. Faust: "Over a lifetime of observation, I have noticed that the farmer who observes the Sabbath day seems to get more done on his farm than he would if he worked seven days. The mechanic will be able to turn out more and better products in six days than in seven. The doctor, the lawyer, the dentist, or the scientist will accomplish more by trying to rest on the Sabbath than if he tries to utilize every day of the week for his professional work. I would counsel all students, if they can, to arrange their schedules so that they do not study on the Sabbath. If students and other seekers after truth will do this, their minds will be quickened and the infinite Spirit will lead them to the verities they wish to learn. This is because God has hallowed his day and blessed it as a perpetual covenant of faithfulness."[15]

CONCLUSION

We live in a rapidly decaying world, in a society that is taking the most direct route to destruction. Because we cannot afford to partake of worldliness, we must seek to do all in our power to acquire and cultivate holiness. "Be ye holy," we have been told, "for I [the Lord] am holy" (1 Peter 1:16; see also Leviticus 11:44). More specifically, "Ye shall keep my sabbaths, and reverence my sanctuary: I am the Lord" (Leviticus 19:30). "But remember that on this, the Lord's day, thou shalt offer thine oblations and thy sacraments unto the Most High, confessing thy sins unto thy brethren, and before the Lord. And on this day thou shalt do none other thing, only let thy food be prepared with singleness of heart that thy fasting" (that is, our hungering and thirsting after righteousness) "may be perfect, or, in other words, that thy joy may be full. Verily, this is fasting and prayer, or in other words, rejoicing and prayer." (D&C 59:12–14.)

One sign and witness to God and to all men and women that we are eager to keep ourselves unspotted from the vices of the world is our willingness to keep the Sabbath day holy. It is a token of holiness, a visible symbol of our desire to honor Jesus Christ, even He who established the Sabbath, "the very Eternal Father of heaven and of earth" (Alma 11:39). I have a conviction that if we strive daily to draw near unto God, through brief but consistent scripture study, pondering, and prayer, that the Sabbath will indeed become the spiritual highlight and capstone of our week, the culmination of a diligent quest for holiness and peace. We thereby qualify for the cleansing and motivating power of the Holy Spirit in our lives and thus enter into the rest of the Lord. The Holy One becomes our God and we become His people, a people of covenant.

Notes

1. Bruce R. McConkie, *The Mortal Messiah* (Salt Lake City: Deseret Book, 1979), 1:201.

2. Brigham Young, in *Journal of Discourses,* 7:138.

3. Joseph F. Smith, *Gospel Doctrine* (Salt Lake City: Deseret Book, 1971), 242, emphasis added.

4. Ibid., 58.

5. Spencer W. Kimball, *The Miracle of Forgiveness* (Salt Lake City: Bookcraft Inc., 1969), 97.

6. Harold B. Lee, *The Teachings of Harold B. Lee* (Salt Lake City: Bookcraft, 1996), 210.

7. David O. McKay, *Gospel Ideals* (Salt Lake City: *Improvement Era,* 1953), 377–98.

8. Mark E. Petersen, *Ensign,* May 1975, 49.

9. George Albert Smith, in Conference Report, October 1935, 120.

10. Spencer W. Kimball, *Ensign,* November 1978, 5.

11. Spencer W. Kimball, *Ensign,* November 1979, 4.

12. Ezra Taft Benson, *The Teachings of Ezra Taft Benson* (Salt Lake City: Bookcraft, 1988), 439.

13. Spencer W. Kimball, *Ensign,* November 1975, 6.

14. Gordon B. Hinckley, speaking at a regional training meeting, as quoted by Earl C. Tingey, *Ensign,* May 1996, 10.

15. James E. Faust, *Finding Light in a Dark World* (Salt Lake City: Deseret Book, 1995), 112.

5

"Honour Thy Father and Thy Mother"

HOYT W. BREWSTER, JR.

*I*N ORDER TO GRASP THE full significance of the fifth commandment, one must recognize the central role of the family unit in God's eternal plan. "Families are forever" is not just a Latter-day Saint slogan to be seen creatively displayed in their homes, or even casually affixed as a bumper sticker. It is a portentous principle with deep theological import.

THE FAMILY IS THE BASIC UNIT IN TIME AND ETERNITY

Before coming to this earth, each human being lived in a premortal family with our Heavenly Father and a Heavenly Mother. Indeed, the deep yet simple "doctrine of the pre-existence," as

*While writing this chapter, **Hoyt W. Brewster, Jr.**, was serving as managing director of the Priesthood Department at the Church offices in Salt Lake City. At the publication of this book, he is serving as president of the Netherlands Amsterdam Mission. He and his wife, Judy, are the parents of five children.*

noted by the First Presidency in 1909, reveals "that man, as a spirit, was begotten and born of heavenly parents, and reared to maturity in the eternal mansions of the Father, prior to coming upon the earth in a temporal body to undergo an experience in mortality."[1]

The most significant decision of that mortal experience comes when, having sought out a worthy companion, one enters with him or her into sacred marital covenants. Latter-day Saints affirm that the relationship of husband and wife can be of an eternal duration. Through the sealing blessings of the holy priesthood of God, as performed by those authorized so to do, the marital union establishes an eternal family unit that can last through time and all eternity *if* the husband and wife are true and faithful to their covenants.

With this introductory perspective on the family in mind, let us consider the circumstances in which the fifth commandment given on Mount Sinai came forth.

THE IMPORTANCE OF THE FAMILY IN ANCIENT ISRAEL

The ancient Israelites were taught to place a high value on the role of parents and the family. Their way of life, including their laws and traditions, revolved around the central place of the family in their society.

Speaking of Jewish beliefs and feelings regarding the family, Elder Bruce R. McConkie commented:

Jewish homes, Jewish family life, the rearing of Jewish children, indeed, the whole Jewish way of life was founded upon Jewish theology. Jehovah's command to children—so basic that it was decree number five in the Decalogue itself—was: "Honour thy father and thy mother: that thy days may be long upon the land which the Lord thy God giveth thee." (Exodus 20:12.) Jehovah's command to parents—so basic that the Jews carried it in their phylacteries, hung it in their Mezuzahs, recited it twice daily in their Shema—was: "Bring up thy children in light and in truth." And that which was to be taught was theological; it was the holy scriptures; it was the mind and will and voice of the Lord to his people. And this is what separated the Jews from all other people.[2]

Of course, the theological underpinnings that sustained the Jewish way of thinking were consistent with those of the other tribes of Israel as well. Each had received the same divine instruction on such matters.

SEVERE PUNISHMENT FOR DISOBEDIENCE TO PARENTS

The importance of respecting and honoring parents was so central to the way of life among the Israelites that young people who violated that code of conduct could be subject to death. Consider, for example, the potential consequences ensuing to the rebellious or disobedient offspring:

> If a man have a stubborn and rebellious son, which will not obey the voice of his father, or the voice of his mother, and that, when they have chastened him, will not hearken unto them:
> Then shall his father and his mother lay hold on him, and bring him out unto the elders of his city and unto the gate of his place;
> And they shall say unto the elders of his city, This our son is stubborn and rebellious, he will not obey our voice; he is a glutton, and a drunkard.
> And all the men of his city shall stone him with stones, that he die; so shalt thou put evil away from among you; and all Israel shall hear, and fear. (Deuteronomy 21:18–21; see also Exodus 21:17; Leviticus 20:9; Matthew 15:4; Mark 7:10.)

Jesus Christ Reiterated the Importance of Honoring Parents

During His mortal ministry, Jesus Christ forcefully reminded the Pharisees and scribes of their neglect of the fifth commandment. "Ye have not kept the ordinances of God," declared He who gave the Decalogue. "For Moses said, Honor thy father and thy mother; and whoso curseth father or mother, let him die the death of the transgressor, as it is written in your law; but ye keep not the law." (JST, Mark 7:12.)

Jesus then chided them for their corrupt use of Corban. Corban was a means of declaring something as a gift intended for or dedicated to God. Such a gift was legally exempt from all other obligations, including the need to provide temporal support for one's parents or other needy family members.

Thus, "according to the rabbinical teachings, a wealthy son could say to destitute parents, 'It is Corban,' and thus be free of his obligation to support them. Originally this had meant, in effect, 'My property is Corban or has been pledged or given to God, and therefore it cannot be used to support you in your poverty.' Then the selfish son could continue to use his property as long as he lived. But by Jesus' day the practice and teaching was so corrupt that Corban meant merely to take a vow; and so by saying, 'It is Corban,' the son meant, 'I have vowed not to support you'; and so he was free of the command to honor his parents, for according to 'the tradition of the elders,' it was more important to keep his vow than obey God and honor his parents."[3]

The Redeemer's ringing rebuke of such a practice was, "Ye suffer him no more to do aught for his father or his mother; making the word of God of none effect through your tradition." (JST, Mark 7:13).

The First Commandment with Promise

It is of interest to note that the fifth commandment has been referred to as "the first commandment with promise" (Ephesians 6:2).[4] The great Jehovah's command "Honour thy father and thy mother" was immediately followed by the promise: "that thy days may be long upon the land which the Lord thy God giveth thee" (Exodus 20:12).

In reflecting on this promise, Elder Dallin H. Oaks of the Quorum of the Twelve Apostles said: "I have wondered about the relationship between the commandment and the promise. How could honoring our parents increase our longevity?"

Elder Oaks then related how in the early days of his marriage he had observed the loving care given by his mother-in-law, True Dixon, to his wife's maternal grandmother, Adelaide White Call. Grandma Call was an aged widow whose days in the twilight of life were made more pleasant because of her inclusion in the activities of her children and their families.

Many years have passed since Elder Oaks observed the tender care provided to one who was experiencing diminished capacity to care for herself and whose own circle of close friends and family members had likewise diminished. However, the fruits of this labor of love continue to be harvested. For now Elder Oaks has seen his wife, June, and her brother and sisters care for their mother in the same loving way she had cared for her mother.

"I believe," declared Elder Oaks, "[my mother-in-law's] days will be longer upon the land because of the attentiveness and companionship of her children, who learned the way to honor a parent by seeing how their own mother honored hers."

He then added: "I am sure that when the time comes, my own companion's days will be lengthened upon the land because of the care her children will give to her because of the example she has set for them. A worthy example repeats itself from generation to generation."[5]

ETERNAL IMPLICATIONS TO HONORING PARENTS

In addition to the lengthening of one's *mortal* days upon this earth, there may well be far more significant implications in an *eternal* perspective.

Consider the Lord's decree that this earth will be an eternal abode that those "who are of the celestial kingdom may possess it forever and ever" (D&C 88:20). Indeed, the Savior has on several occasions declared, "Blessed are the meek, for they shall inherit the [celestialized] earth" (Matthew 5:5; 3 Nephi 12:5; see also D&C 88:17).

Certainly, those who truly honor their parents through righteous living and keeping sacred covenants are among the meek who will inherit this earth. Not only will their days be long upon the land of their inheritance—the celestialized earth—but they will become heirs of all the promised blessings pronounced upon the great patriarch Abraham. Such blessings include the promise of "eternal lives," or the promise of a never-ending posterity. (See Abraham 2:6–11; D&C 132:29–50.)

Is not the extending of one's posterity another means of extending one's days?

WE HONOR PARENTS AS WE HONOR OUR ANCESTORS

The commandment to honor one's parents should not be myopically viewed with one-generational lenses, but must rightly be seen as extending to one's ancestors as well. Indeed, how can we truly honor our parents if we do not also honor our parents' parents and their parents, continuing back to the first parents of the human family, even Adam and Eve?

One means whereby we can honor our ancestors is to live in such a way that we keep our names unblemished from anything that would bring dishonor to them. Indeed, our very names may be a constant reminder to us of that often-heard admonition loving parents give to children who are leaving for an evening of fun and social activity: "Remember who you are!" (What is generally left unspoken, but surely understood, is the second phrase—"And act accordingly!")

Consider the counsel given by one father to sons who had been given the names of their worthy forefathers: "Behold, I have given unto you the names of our first parents who came out of the land of Jerusalem; and this I have done that when you remember your names ye may remember them; and when ye remember them ye may remember their works; and when ye remember their works ye may know how that it is said, and also written, that they were good" (Helaman 5:6).

Surely a name is a trust given for safekeeping. When eternal reunions occur, as each of us takes his or her turn at passing through the veil of mortal death, our hope should be to greet our ancestors with the joyful knowledge that we have kept their names clean and worthy to pass on to our children and the generations that follow us.

On one occasion President Spencer W. Kimball spoke of the deep respect he and his family held for their noble grandfather, Heber C. Kimball. Brother Kimball was described as "unwavering in his devotion to the Lord and in his determination to keep the commandments."

Said President Kimball of his grandfather: "We are rightly proud to be his children, but that great heritage is a challenge to us to measure up. None of us now living knew Grandfather, but we shall meet him, perhaps sooner than we expect. What a pleasure that will be, especially if we can report that we have brought honor to the family name!"[6]

WE HONOR PARENTS BY TURNING OUR HEARTS TO OUR ANCESTORS

There is yet another means of honoring our parents that has its roots deep in Latter-day Saint theology. One of the prophecies cited by the heavenly messenger Moroni, in his nocturnal visit to the Prophet Joseph Smith in September of 1823, was that of the prophet Malachi (see Malachi 4:5–6).

Moroni's recitation of this prophecy was slightly different from the way it is presently recorded in the last two verses of the Old Testament and was uttered as follows:

"Behold, I will reveal unto you the Priesthood, by the hand of Elijah the prophet, before the coming of the great and dreadful day of the Lord. And he shall plant in the hearts of the children the promises made to the fathers, and the hearts of the children shall turn to their fathers. If it were not so, the whole earth would be utterly wasted at his coming." (D&C 2:1–3; see also Joseph Smith-History 1:38–39.)

Almost thirteen years from the time Moroni quoted this prophecy it was fulfilled, for Elijah the resurrected prophet was sent to restore the sealing keys to the Prophet Joseph Smith in the Kirtland Temple (see D&C 110:13–16).

How have the hearts of the children been turned to their fathers?

In answer, I quote a previously published statement of mine: "To turn one's heart to the fathers is to seek after one's dead, and to perform the saving ordinances of the gospel in their behalf."[7]

In what greater way can one honor ancestors than by searching out their names and performing by proxy essential saving ordinances in their behalf? The Prophet Joseph Smith warned that "the earth will be smitten with a curse unless there is a welding link of some kind or other between the fathers and the children. . . . For we without them cannot be made perfect; neither can they without us be made perfect." (D&C 128:18.)

Thus I repeat an earlier statement: The commandment to honor one's parents should not be myopically viewed with one-generational lenses, but must rightly be seen as extending to one's ancestors as well.

WE HONOR OUR HEAVENLY PARENTS BY HONORING OUR EARTHLY PARENTS

By extending the blessings of God's plan of salvation to our ancestors, we honor our Heavenly Parents; for in so doing we assist our Heavenly Father in carrying out His declared purpose to "bring to pass the immortality and eternal life of man" (Moses 1:39).

Furthermore, as we live in accordance with the righteous instructions given us by our earthly parents, we honor our Heavenly Parents as well. Certainly there is joy in our heavenly home when the actions of righteous children create joy in earthly homes. Consider how the words of praise by a mortal father to his faithful son were undoubtedly echoed by Heavenly Father: "And now, my son, I trust that I shall have great joy in you, because of your steadiness and your faithfulness unto God. . . . I say unto you, my son, that I have had great joy in thee already, because of thy faithfulness." (Alma 38:2–3.)

Contrast the joy brought to parents of righteous children with the sorrow experienced by parents of rebellious children. For example, Nephi described the suffering caused his parents by the disobedience of some of their children as follows: "And my parents being stricken in years, and having suffered much grief because of their children, they were brought down, yea, even upon their sick-beds" (1 Nephi 18:17).

We probably cannot imagine the deep sorrow our Heavenly Parents must feel when their children rebel and act contrary to their divine nature.

THE COMMANDMENT TO HONOR PARENTS IS A CHALLENGE TO RIGHTEOUS LIVING

It appears that complete compliance with the fifth commandment would really cover compliance with the other nine as well. This same statement could be made of the first commandment as well, for by fully worshipping, loving, and honoring God, one would be sure not to break any of His other commandments. Thus the commandments to honor God and parents are inextricably interwoven.

Elder Dallin H. Oaks said: "The commandment to honor our parents has strands that run through the entire fabric of the gospel. It is inherent in our relationship to God our Father. It embraces the divine destiny of the children of God."[8]

In essence, the commandment to honor one's parents is a challenge to righteous living.

The words of President Spencer W. Kimball provide a good summary statement: "If we truly honor [our parents], we will seek to emulate their best characteristics and to fulfill their highest aspirations for us. No gift purchased from a store can begin to match in value to parents some simple, sincere words of appreciation. Nothing we could give them would be more prized than righteous living for each youngster."[9]

Notes

1. "The Origin of Man," in James R. Clark, comp., *Messages of the First Presidency*, 6 vols. (Salt Lake City: Bookcraft, 1965–1975), 4:205.

2. *The Mortal Messiah*, 4 vols. (Salt Lake City: Deseret Book Co., 1979–1981), 1:225.

3. Bruce R. McConkie, *Doctrinal New Testament Commentary*, 3 vols. (Salt Lake City: Bookcraft, 1965–73), 1:367.

4. See also Conference Reports, October 1959, 101; April 1965, 71.

5. *Ensign*, May 1991, 17.

6. Edward L. Kimball, ed., *The Teachings of Spencer W. Kimball* (Salt Lake City: Bookcraft, 1982), 348.

7. Hoyt W. Brewster, Jr., *Doctrine & Covenants Encyclopedia* (Salt Lake City: Bookcraft, 1988), 236.

8. *Ensign*, May 1991, 15.

9. *The Teachings of Spencer W. Kimball*, 348.

6

"Thou Shalt Not Kill"

WAYNE R. DYMOCK

LIFE AND THE AGENCY TO DIRECT that life are sacred. Man in the premortal spirit world was the spirit offspring of Deity. To help bring about His "plan of salvation" for all of His children, our Heavenly Father caused this earth to be created and provided the opportunity for each of us to receive a mortal body. The spirit and the body together help to bring a fulness of joy (see D&C 93:33–34). The crowning act of all God's creation was man. "So God created man in his own image, in the image of God created he him; male and female created he them" (Genesis 1: 27). One of the greatest affronts to God himself is the destruction of that life. "Whoso sheddeth man's blood, by man shall his blood be shed: *for in the image of God made he man*" (Genesis 9:6; emphasis added). To destroy a human life is to sin against God and His plan. Note the words of Elder Harold B. Lee on this subject:

Wayne R. Dymock is an instructor at the Logan Institute of Religion at Utah State University and serves in the bishopric of his ward. He and his wife, Julie, are the parents of five children.

One of the most serious of all sins and crimes against the Lord's plan of salvation is the sin of murder or the destruction of human life. It seems clear that to be guilty of destroying life is the act of "rebellion" against the plan of the Almighty by denying an individual thus destroyed in mortality, the privilege of a full experience in this earth-school of opportunity. It is in the same category as the rebellion of Satan and his hosts and therefore it would not be surprising if the penalties to be imposed upon a murderer were to be of similar character as the penalties meted out to those spirits which were cast out of heaven with Satan.[1]

Topping the list of commandments dealing with our fellowmen is the commandment "Thou shalt not kill" (Exodus 20:13). In the New Testament account of Christ and the rich young man, Jesus admonished him to keep all the commandments. In reviewing these commandments, He stated "thou shalt do no murder" (Matthew 19:18). Indeed, the Hebrew word *hārag*, translated "kill" in the King James Version, can also be translated "murder" and means "to slay, smite, put to death, slaughter, let die."[2]

When Jehovah gave Israel the Decalogue from Mount Sinai, it was by no means the first time man was forbidden to shed another man's blood. Cain killed his brother Abel to gain the latter's flocks. The scriptures record that the blood from this first murder "cries unto me from the ground" for vengeance (Genesis 4:10, Moses 5:35). Cursed by God, Cain stated that his punishment was "greater than I can bear" (Moses 5:38). President Spencer W. Kimball wrote of Cain: "For Cain suffered far more than did Abel, and murder is far more serious to him who commits it than to him who suffers from it."[3] After the Flood, as Noah began a new "genesis" of mankind, the Lord again revealed "surely your blood of your lives will I require . . . at the hand of man," and forbade the shedding of man's blood (see Genesis 9:5–6).

The scriptures record that during the dispensation led by Moses there were additional instructions and "case laws" dealing with killing. Wilful murder was distinguished from accidental homicide, and was invariably visited with capital punishment (see Numbers 35:16, 18, 21, 31; Leviticus 24:17). The "avenger of blood" was the nearest relative of the murdered, and was required to avenge his death (Numbers 35:24, 27). The Mosaic law prohibited any compensation for murder or the reprieve of the murderer (see Exodus 21:12, 14; Deuteronomy 19:11–13; 2 Samuel 20:10). Two witnesses were required in any capital case (see Numbers 35:19–30; Deuteronomy 17:6–12). If the murderer could not be discovered, the city nearest the scene of the murder was required to make expiation for the crime committed (Deuteronomy 21:1–9).

The Book of Mormon also testifies that the blood of the Saints and the innocent cry up from the ground for vengeance (see Mosiah 17:19; Alma 1:13; Ether 8:22), and especially the blood of the murdered prophets (see Alma 37:30). In our own dispensation, in America, we have witnessed the result of killing the Lord's prophet. Seventeen years after Joseph and Hyrum were murdered in Carthage Jail, this nation was embroiled in a war that took more lives than any war we have fought since.

THE SERIOUS SIN OF MURDER

Murder is second in seriousness only to the sin against the Holy Ghost. Elder George Q. Cannon in a conference address said that "He [God] had made murder the worst crime that could be committed by man against his fellow man."[4] Elder B. H. Roberts also wrote ". . . on the crime of murder is placed the heaviest of all penalties—'whoso sheddeth man's blood, by man shall his blood be shed.'(Genesis 9:6)"[5] Reasons for its seriousness include the fact that murder robs its victims of the opportunity to work out their salvation. Repentance requires restitution, but it is impossible for a person to restore the life of another. Murder also impacts the lives of those connected to its victims.

The *Encyclopedia of Mormonism* states: "The Church defines 'murder' as the deliberate and unjustified taking of human life."[6]

Elder Bruce R. McConkie defines and states the seriousness of this sin in the following statement:

> Murder, the unlawful killing of a human being with malice aforethought or under such circumstances of criminality that the malice is presumed, "is a sin unto death" (1 John 5:16–17), a sin for which there is "no forgiveness" (D.&C. 42:79), meaning that a murderer can never gain salvation. "No murderer hath eternal life abiding in him." (1 John 3:15.) He cannot join the Church by baptism; he is outside the pale of redeeming grace.[7]

Elder McConkie later explained the phrase "sin unto death":

> What are sins unto death? We can answer this only in part. "Thou shalt not kill; and he that kills shall not have forgiveness in this world, nor in the world to come." (D&C 42:18.) Murder is thus a sin unto death, *at least concerning members of the Church,* to whom this revelation, which is entitled "the law of the Church," was addressed. We do know that there are murders committed by Gentiles for which they at least can repent, be baptized, and receive a remission of their sins. (See 3 Nephi 30:1–2.)[8]

For members of the Church who commit murder, the doctrine seems clear: there is no forgiveness in this life or in the world to come. This means the atonement of Christ does not cover the sin of murder for those of covenant Israel who commit this serious sin. The law of justice will extract from the sinner the full price demanded. King David knew such was the case and pleaded with the Lord many days. But he also knew that when the price was paid, the Lord would "not leave my soul in hell" (Psalm 16:10). Peter, speaking on the day of Pentecost, testified that David's body was still in his tomb after Christ's resurrection, but would come forth in a later resurrection (see Acts 2:25–36). As Elder McConkie suggested, the Atonement may cover murder committed by Gentiles. The Anti-Nephi-Lehies, who killed because of the "traditions of their fathers" (Alma 23:3), were freed from the curse and entered into a covenant with God. This judgment as to whether a person who has committed murder may be baptized into the Church is made by the First Presidency. The position of the Church is stated in the following:

> Secular punishment for killing is to be proved and "dealt with according to the laws of the land" (D&C 42:79). Those who have been convicted of, or have confessed to, homicide cannot be baptized without clearance from the First Presidency, and excommunication of members guilty of murder is mandatory. Joseph Fielding Smith, as an apostle, indicated that vicarious temple work should not be done for deceased murderers (DS 2:192).[9]

President Spencer W. Kimball also stated:

> Occasionally people who have murdered come to the Church requesting baptism, having come to some partial realization of the enormity of the crime. Missionaries do not knowingly baptize such people. Rather than assuming this great responsibility, they refer the problem to their mission presidents who in turn will wish to refer the matter to the First Presidency of the Church.[10]

The fact still remains that those who murder will need to repent of their sin. After spending time in that portion of the spirit world called "hell," they will be reformed and they will come forth worthy to enter the telestial kingdom (see D&C 76: 81–91). Again, the words of President Spencer W. Kimball give added insights to the need for murderers to repent:

> Even unpardonable sins should be repented of. The murderer does not have eternal life abiding in him, but a merciful God will grant to every soul adequate rewards for every good

deed he does. God is just. He will compensate for every effort to do good, to repent, to overcome sin. Even the murderer is justified in repenting and mending his ways and building up a credit balance in his favor.[11]

DEGREES OF MURDER

Life can be taken in many ways. The laws of man recognize that sometimes life is taken with forethought and evil intent, and at other times in anger without intent to kill. President Kimball explained it in these words:

> Even among wilful murderers there are grades and categories. There are the Herods and the Eichmanns and the Heydrichs, who kill for sadistic pleasure. There are those who kill in drunkenness, in rage, in anger, in jealousy. There are those who kill for gain, for power, for fear. There are those who kill for lust. They certainly will suffer different degrees of punishment hereafter. The proper earthly penalty for the crime is clearly set out in the scriptures and applied to all ages of the world. This penalty is the prerogative and responsibility of governmental authority, since no unauthorized person may take the law into his own hands and slay a fellow being.[12]

Sometimes death is caused by the carelessness, neglect, or reckless actions of another. How responsible is a person in this case? What about people who kill as a result of medications they may be taking that clouds their judgment? This statement from the *Encyclopedia of Mormonism* gives insight:

> If death is caused by carelessness or by defense of self or others, or if overriding mitigating circumstances prevail (such as deficient mental capacity or state of war), the taking of a human life may be regarded as something other than murder. In making the assessment of a member's guilt or innocence of murder, Church leaders are encouraged to be responsive to

inspiration and to submit the facts of the case to the office of the First Presidency for review. In the final analysis, only God, who can discern the thoughts of the heart, can judge whether a particular killing is an unforgivable murder or not.[13]

THE PENALTIES FOR MURDER

From the scriptures we learn that "He that smiteth a man, so that he die, shall be surely put to death" (Exodus 21:12). And "he that killeth any man shall surely be put to death" (Leviticus 24:17). From modern revelation: "Thou shalt not kill, but he that killeth shall die" (D&C 42:19). In the Doctrine and Covenants the Lord has revealed his "law" to the Church in the last days. Otten and Caldwell have outlined in their commentary the penalties of the law as it related to members of the Church who murder. Note:

> When a member of the Church is guilty of wilfully taking the life of another child of God, the Lord's law specifies three penalties:
>   a.   He shall not obtain forgiveness for his sin in this world or in the world to come (see D&C 42:18). This means he will not have access to the redeeming powers of the Savior's atonement. He will bear the entire burden of this sin.
>   b.   The murderer shall die (see D&C 42:19).
>   c.   He shall be delivered to and dealt with by the laws of the land (see D&C 42:79).[14]

With regard to capital punishment for those committing murder, the Church has long held the position that "a

> person convicted of murder by a lawful government may be subject to the death penalty. The Church generally has not objected to capital punishment legally and justly administered. Indeed, scriptural records both ancient and modern condone

such punishment (Genesis 9:5–6; Exodus 21:12, 23; 2 Nephi 9:35; Alma 1:13–14; D&C 42:19).[15]

THE QUESTION OF WAR

There are many questions that naturally arise about the sixth commandment and war. Do those who go to battle break the sixth commandment? Is it still possible to commit murder on the battlefield? Who is responsible for the deaths of so many killed during times of war? The prophets have not left us in the dark concerning these grave matters. Note the following statements on war and murder.

From Elder Spencer W. Kimball:

Men unfortunately must take others' lives in war. Some of our conscientious young men have been disturbed and concerned as they have been compelled to kill. There are mitigating circumstances but certainly the blame and responsibility rest heavily upon the heads of those who brought about the war, making necessary the taking of life. It is conceivable that even in war there may be many times when there is a legitimate choice and enemy combatants could be taken prisoner rather than be killed.[16]

Further clarification has been given by the Church concerning indiscriminate killing during war in this statement:

The Church also leaves open the possibility that under some unusual circumstances, standard justifications for killing that would normally relieve the individual from responsibility for murder, such as self-defense or defense of others, may not apply automatically. Wartime military service is considered a mitigating factor, not a justification for indiscriminate killing, thus suggesting that even in warfare one's conduct is measured and weighed by God and is not a matter of license.[17]

Under Moses, the Lord outlined the laws for soldiers and for making war in the Israelites' circumstances (see Deuteronomy 20). During times of war the prophets gathered the people, offered sacrifices, and sought the Lord's will whether Israel should go to battle. If the Lord sanctioned their going up against their enemies, Israel was to go to battle in the strength of the Lord, for "the Lord your God is he that goeth with you, to fight for you" (Deuteronomy 20:4). Over time, the prophets were rejected or killed and Israel went to battle in God's name but without His blessing. One has to wonder how many battles have been fought in God's name, but without His approval. President J. Reuben Clark addressed this very concern:

> Nothing is more unrighteous, more unholy, more un-Godly, than man-declared mass slaughter of his fellowman for an unrighteous cause. It has brought down the wrath of the Almighty in all times. God will visit His vengeance upon all who bring it. The law declared at Sinai was "Thou shalt not kill," and in the Garden of Gethsemane: "All they that take the sword shall perish with the sword." With these divine commands deep-embodied in our spiritual consciousness, we can look with no degree of allowance upon the sin of unholy war, and a war to make conquest or to keep conquest already made is such a war.[18]

Orson F. Whitney shed light on why the Lord called the house of Israel into battle:

> Joshua's war upon the Canaanites was a just war, designed to rid the earth of a corrupt generation, which had forfeited its right to longer remain, encumbering the soil, particularly that part which the Creator and Owner of the planet had given to a worthier people. Jehovah's command to clear the ground upon which he proposed erecting a national structure that should stand as a temple of wisdom and light for all succeeding generations, did not impinge upon any command of his

previously given. Neither is the Divine One amenable to human judgment. "Thou shalt not kill" was a commandment from God, not *to* him. His word is superior to all human enactments and to all man's notions of right and wrong. The war waged by Joshua and the hosts of Israel against the wicked and usurping Canaanites was in every respect justifiable, so far as it was conducted according to Jehovah's command.[19]

The Prophet Joseph Smith taught that the government of heaven is based on revelation and related it to the question of war:

God said, "Thou shalt not kill;" at another time He said, "Thou shalt utterly destroy." This is the principle on which the government of heaven is conducted—by revelation adapted to the circumstances in which the children of the kingdom are placed. Whatever God requires is right, no matter what it is, although we may not see the reason thereof till long after the events transpire. If we seek first the kingdom of God, all good things will be added.[20]

During World War II, the First Presidency issued several statements on and about war. They provided great comfort and direction to the Saints at a very critical time. They condemned war and yet held out hope for those called into battle. I quote from two of their statements:

But all these commands, from Sinai down, run in very terms against individuals as members of society, as well as members of the Church, for one man must not kill another as Cain killed Abel; they also run against the Church as in the case of securing land in Zion, because Christ's Church should not make war, for the Lord is a Lord of peace. He has said to us in this dispensation: "Therefore, renounce war and proclaim peace." (D&C 98:16.)

Thus the Church is and must be against war. The Church itself cannot wage war, unless and until the Lord shall issue new commands. It cannot regard war as a righteous means of settling international disputes; these should and could be settled—the nations agreeing—by peaceful negotiation and adjustment.[21]

When, therefore, constitutional law, obedient to these principles, calls the manhood of the Church into the armed service of any country to which they owe allegiance, their highest civic duty requires that they meet that call. If, hearkening to that call and obeying those in command over them, they shall take the lives of those who fight against them, that will not make of them murderers, nor subject them to the penalty that God has prescribed for those who kill, beyond the principle to be mentioned shortly. For it would be a cruel God that would punish His children as moral sinners for acts done by them as the innocent instrumentalities of a sovereign whom He had told them to obey and whose will they were powerless to resist.

The whole world is in the midst of a war that seems the worst of all time. This Church is a worldwide Church. Its devoted members are in both camps. They are the innocent war instrumentalities of their warring sovereignties. On each side they believe they are fighting for home, and country, and freedom. On each side, our brethren pray to the same God, in the same name, for victory. Both sides cannot be wholly right; perhaps neither is without wrong. God will work out in His own due time and in His own sovereign way the justice and right of the conflict, but He will not hold the innocent instrumentalities of the war, our brethren in arms, responsible for the conflict. This is a major crisis in the world-life of man. God is at the helm.[22]

"Whoso is Angry"—Living the Higher Law

In the meridian of time Christ came among men to fulfill the law He had given to ancient Israel. He then gave men His higher laws. In what is known as the Sermon on the Mount, Jesus said: "Ye have heard that it was said by them of old time, Thou shalt not kill; and whosoever shall kill shall be in danger of the judgment: but I say unto you, That whosoever is angry with his brother without a cause shall be in danger of the judgment: and whosoever shall say to his brother, Raca, shall be in danger of the council: but whosoever shall say, Thou fool, shall be in danger of hell fire" (Matthew 5:21–22).

The Apostle John would later record: "Whosoever hateth his brother is a murderer: and ye know that no murderer hath eternal life abiding in him" (1 John 3:15). Anger has led many individuals to take life when they would not have thought it possible. Nephi told us that in our day Satan would "rage in the hearts of the children of men, and stir them up to anger" (2 Nephi 28:20). Greediness, seeking revenge, and giving offenses all stir men up to anger. Elder Bruce R. McConkie wrote about anger in the following words:

> Moses' law—more properly Jehovah's law given through Moses—forbade murder. "Thou shalt not kill; and whosoever shall kill, shall be in danger of the judgment of God." The same prohibition applies under the gospel law, but this higher law, in addition, raises a higher standard. It strikes at the cause of murder, which is anger. The man whose fired bullet misses its human target is as guilty as the marksman whose bullet brings death to the intended victim. It is the feeling one has in his heart that counts, not the eventuality that occurs.[23]

Hugh Nibley provides some unique insights to anger and shows how Satan has taken a God-given emotion and used it for his purposes:

The next point Jesus says, again turning to the old and bringing about the new, "Ye have heard that it hath been said by them of old time, and it is also written before you [the Nephites had these records, of course, in writing as well] that thou shalt not kill." Jesus then said: I don't want any anger; I don't want any ridicule; I don't want evil speaking. Why is this so important? Why does this amount to the equivalent in significance of murder under the old rule? Well, the Lord placed enmity in this world for one reason, and one reason only. Hatred is here so that we can hate evil. What does the devil do with that enmity? He says, fine—all right, God, you have let evil into the world; then I will take that evil and with it I will make people hate one another. He misdirects our hatred and our anger—a typical strategy that Satan is going to try to employ. Jesus says if we are going to reverse that, we've got to rid our lives of anger and hostility, especially toward a brother. It says you can't call another *Raca* (fool). It's a derisive word, laughing at what he is doing. Why? When you laugh at a brother or a sister in whom resides the spirit of God, you are ridiculing God himself. The early Christians taught that doctrine, and for that reason you have councils referred to in the early Christian literature where people were brought before the council because they had spoken evil of one another. This was grounds for excommunication. This is worse than death itself. Why? Because it reviles and defies God and his presence in the community that is being formed.[24]

Finally, President Kimball also shows how anger can lead to murder and encourages us to avoid the steps leading to it: "Much better is it to avoid the steps which lead to unforgivable sin. Thus as a preventive measure against murder one should avoid anger and hatred, avarice and greed, and any of the other impulses which can spark the act. Nephi said his brothers were murderers at heart. One usually will commit the deed in his thoughts many times before he will deliberately commit the crime in actuality."[25]

KILLING OF ANIMALS

As a young man growing up on a small farm, I was around many different kinds of animals. My father instilled in me early a reverence for all types of life. Many hours were spent caring for and feeding the animals. I saw mothers care for their newborn, sense when there was danger, and do what they could to care for and protect their young. Occasionally, some of the animals were killed to provide meat for our family. As I helped in the process, my father would explain why God provided animal life, and the importance to give thanks to Him for the animal who helped to meet our needs.

I had many friends growing up who, for fun, would go hunt birds or the many jackrabbits we had native to the area. I knew this would displease my father, but I also never felt motivated to go. I will never forget going to a general priesthood meeting at our stake center and hearing President Kimball give his talk on not killing the little birds. It reinforced what I knew and had been taught. I quote from a part of his words:

> I read at the priesthood meeting at the last conference the words to the verse of the song years ago, "Don't Kill the Little Birds," with which I was familiar when I was a child growing up in Arizona. I found many young boys around my age who, with their flippers and their slings, destroyed many birds. . . .
>
> Now, I also would like to add some of my feelings concerning the unnecessary shedding of blood and destruction of life. I think that every soul should be impressed by the sentiments that have been expressed here by the prophets.
>
> And not less with reference to the killing of innocent birds is the wildlife of our country that live upon the vermin that are indeed enemies to the farmer and to mankind. It is not only wicked to destroy them, it is a shame, in my opinion. I think that this principle should extend not only to the bird life but to the life of all animals. For that purpose I read the scripture where the Lord gave us all the animals. Seemingly,

he thought it was important that all these animals be on the earth for our use and encouragement.[26]

Joseph F. Smith also spoke on this subject: "I do not believe any man should kill animals or birds unless he needs them for food, and then he should not kill innocent little birds that are not intended for food for man. I think it is wicked for men to thirst in their souls to kill almost everything which possesses animal life. It is wrong, and I have been surprised at prominent men whom I have seen whose very souls seemed to be athirst for the shedding of animal blood."[27]

As a Varsity Scout coach I took a group of boys hiking up in the mountains. We had been told there were many rattlesnakes in the area where we were hiking.

That afternoon we came across two rattlesnakes near the creek. I watched to see the reaction of the boys. Almost every one of them picked up a rock or stick to kill them. I had come prepared for the moment and called for a coach's minute. The boys huddled around, and I shared the experience Joseph Smith had as part of Zion's camp:

We crossed the Embarras river and encamped on a small branch of the same about one mile west. In pitching my tent we found three massasaugas or prairie rattlesnakes, which the brethren were about to kill, but I said, "Let them alone— don't hurt them! How will the serpent ever lose his venom, while the servants of God possess the same disposition and continue to make war upon it? Men must become harmless, before the brute creation; and when men lose their vicious dispositions and cease to destroy the animal race, the lion and the lamb can dwell together, and the sucking child can play with the serpent in safety." The brethren took the serpents carefully on sticks and carried them across the creek. I exhorted the brethren not to kill a serpent, bird, or an animal of any kind during our journey unless it became necessary in order to preserve ourselves from hunger.[28]

Things "Like Unto It"

The sixth commandment is violated in many ways in society today. Newspaper and television headlines abound with stories of killing and murder. We hear and see accounts of genocide, mass murders, "ethnic cleansing," and gang-related drive-by shootings. In our dispensation the Lord has commanded us to not kill, and He then added these words, "nor do anything like unto it" (D&C 59:6). Issues such as abortion, suicide, knowingly transmitting AIDS, mercy killing, and toxic pollution certainly fit the "like unto it" postscript. These issues are symptoms of the breakdown of our society and the "forgetting" of God and His plan. Let us briefly examine some of these "like unto it" issues.

Computer and Arcade Games

I remember once attending a seminary fireside where the speaker spoke to our youth about some of the computer and arcade type games on the market. I have long since forgotten the name of that speaker, but not his message. He said that these games could be labeled "thou shalt not kill, nor do anything like unto it." One particular game had the Americans pitted against the Russians. He went on to remind these youth that the Russians were our brothers and sisters, and that we needed to take the gospel to them, not pretend to destroy them. Since he gave that talk, we have all witnessed the fall of communism and the spread of the gospel to this great people.

TV and Movies

The movie and television industries offer increasingly more graphic and explicit violence. Murder is glorified before our eyes. Many of our children have seen thousands of murders acted out on the screen, numbing them to the seriousness of the act. I had a young Japanese exchange student visit my seminary class one day. She agreed to entertain a few questions from the class. When asked what was the major difference between the people of America and Japan she replied, "Americans are very violent." We were all humbled and shocked that she perceived something we had not realized was affecting us. No wonder, when we have such a steady diet of violence on televion and in our movies. We need to learn from the past, for in the days of Noah, "the earth was filled with violence" (Genesis 6:13), and God destroyed man by the Flood.

Abortion

In 1985, Elder Russell M. Nelson, of the Council of the Twelve, addressed the Church in general conference about the issue of abortion. He called it "a new war that *annually* claims more casualties than the total number of fatalities from all the wars of this nation".[29] Some 55 million abortions were reported in 1974 throughout the world as a means of convenience and a form of birth control.[30] The position of the Church has always been against this action:

> The ultimate act of destruction is to take a life. That is why abortion is such a serious sin. Our attitude toward abortion is not based on revealed knowledge of when mortal life begins for legal purposes. It is fixed by our knowledge that according to an eternal plan, all of the spirit children of God must come to this earth for a glorious purpose, and that individual identity began long before conception and will continue for all the eternities to come. We rely on the prophets of God, who have told us that while there may be "rare" exceptions, "the practice of elective abortion is fundamentally contrary to the Lord's injunction, "Thou shalt not . . . kill, nor do anything like unto it" (Doctrine and Covenants 59:6). (*1991 Supplement to the 1989 General Handbook of Instructions,* p. 1).[31]

Suicide

Sometimes called "self-murder," suicide is claiming more and more victims each year. Elder M. Russell Ballard, of the Council of the Twelve, addressed this very sensitive subject in an article he wrote for the *Ensign* entitled "Suicide: Some Things We Know and Some We Do Not." He draws this important conclusion:

> I draw an important conclusion from the words of the Prophet: Suicide is a sin—a very grievous one, yet the Lord will not judge the person who commits that sin strictly by the act itself. The Lord will look at that person's circumstances and the degree of his accountability at the time of the act. Of course, this gives us no reason to excuse ourselves in committing sins, nor will the Lord excuse us, if I understand correctly. We must constantly strive to do our best in emulating the Savior in every aspect of our lives.[32]

Elder Bruce R. McConkie has given us this definition and explanation about suicide:

> Suicide consists in the voluntary and intentional taking of one's own life, particularly where the person involved is accountable and has a sound mind. Mortal life is a gift of God; it comes according to the divine will, is appointed to endure for such time as Deity decrees, and is designed to serve as the chief testing period of man's eternal existence. It is the probationary state or time during which man is tried and tested physically, spiritually, and mentally. No man has the right to run away from these tests, no matter how severe they may be, by taking his own life. Obviously persons subject to great stresses may lose control of themselves and become mentally clouded to the point that they are no longer accountable for their acts. Such are not to be condemned for taking their own lives. It should also be remembered that judgment is the Lord's; he knows the thoughts, intents, and

abilities of men; and he in his infinite wisdom will make all things right in due course.[33]

In some cultures, those committing suicide are not allowed funeral service or a proper burial. In the LDS faith: "The body of a person who has committed suicide is not dishonored. If the person has been endowed and otherwise is in good standing with the Church, the body may be buried in temple clothes. Normal funeral procedures are followed."[34]

Euthanasia

There is a growing controversy about the practice of so-called "mercy killing." The debate is intense and the issue has reached the United States Supreme Court. Suffering is viewed as a great evil. The merciful thing to do is to let the sufferer or others take his life. The Church teaches that there is purpose in suffering and that we do not have the right to take life. Note the following statement:

> A person who participates in euthanasia—the deliberate, intentional putting to death of a person suffering from incurable conditions or diseases—violates the commandments of God. There is a difference between *allowing* a terminally ill person to die of natural causes and the *initiating* of action that causes someone's death. The application or denial of life-support systems must be decided reverently, usually by competent and responsible family members through prayer and the consultation of competent medical authorities. It is not wrong to ask the Lord, if it be his will, to shorten the physical suffering of a person whose afflictions are terminal and irreversible.[35]

CONCLUSION

Life is a gift from our Heavenly Father. It is sacred. How we treat our fellowman is a reflection of how we feel towards God in whose image we were created. "Thou shalt not kill" is a law based upon these principles. Elder Lynn A. Mickelsen said:

> "Thou shalt not kill." We are created in the image of God. The union of the flesh with the spirit can bring us a fullness of joy. Teach your children to respect the sanctity of human life, to revere it and cherish it. Human life is the precious stepping-stone to eternal life, and we must jealously guard it from the moment of conception.[36]

The sixth commandment is one of the more violated commandments of our time. Oh that we could have a new Sinai aflame with fire and all the earth could hear again from Jehovah himself the words: "Thou shalt not kill". Let us as a people cherish life and teach our children to love God and those He has created. I conclude with words of counsel from Elder George Albert Smith:

> "Thou shalt not kill." Many people in the world do not seem to realize what a terrible crime it is to take human life. When they become angry, for justifiable reasons as they think, they do not hesitate to destroy human life. Sometimes a life is taken in order that money or property may be seized. And yet there is no crime that a human being can commit that will so far alienate him from the blessings of eternal life in the celestial kingdom as murder. No other crime is equal to it. I think that it is our privilege in this Church, to teach our children, while in their tender years and while they are growing up, the enormity of the crime of taking human life. I feel that our Heavenly Father would justify this people if we would stress, if I may be permitted to use that term, in our homes and in our chapels the sacredness of human life, and the seriousness and importance of living, and cause these boys and girls who are growing up to understand how terrible it would be to commit the awful crime of murder, so that they would not be tempted under any condition so to do.[37]

Notes

1. Harold B. Lee, *The Ten Commandments Today* (Salt Lake City: Deseret Book, 1955), 88.

2. *The International Standard Bible Encyclopedia,* ed. Geoffrey W. Bromiley (Grand Rapids: William B. Eerdmans Publishing Company, 1986), 3:15.

3. Spencer W. Kimball, *The Teachings of Spencer W. Kimball,* ed. Edward L. Kimball (Salt Lake City: Bookcraft, 1982), 188.

4. George Q. Cannon, in Conference Report, April 1899, 67.

5. B. H. Roberts, *The Seventies Course in Theology,* Second Year (Salt Lake City: *Deseret News,* 1980), 38.

6. *Encyclopedia of Mormonism,* s.v. "Murder," 2:970–71.

7. Bruce R. McConkie, *Mormon Doctrine,* 2 ed. rd. (Salt Lake City: Bookcraft, 1966), 520.

8. Bruce R. McConkie, *A New Witness for the Articles of Faith* (Salt Lake City: Deseret Book, 1985), 231, emphasis added.

9. *Encyclopedia of Mormonism,* 2:970–71.

10. Spencer W. Kimball, *The Miracle of Forgiveness* (Salt Lake City: Bookcraft, 1969), 130.

11. Ibid., 131.

12. Ibid., 129–30.

13. *Encyclopedia of Mormonism,* 2:970–71.

14. Otten & Caldwell, *Sacred Truths of the Doctrine & Covenants,* (Lemb. Inc., 1982), 1:199.

15. *Encyclopedia of Mormonism,* 2:970–71.

16. Spencer W. Kimball, *The Miracle of Forgiveness,* 129.

17. *Encyclopedia of Mormonism,* 2:971.

18. J. Reuben Clark, Jr., in Conference Report, October 1939, 11.

19. Orson F. Whitney, *Saturday Night Thoughts,* 181.

20. *Teachings of the Prophet Joseph Smith,* comp. Joseph Fielding Smith (Salt Lake City: Deseret Book, 1976), 256.

21. James R. Clark, comp., *Messages of the First Presidency,* 6:158.

22. Ibid., 159

23. Bruce R. McConkie, *The Mortal Messiah* (Salt Lake City: Deseret Book, 1980), 2:135.

24. Hugh Nibley, *Teachings of the Book of Mormon* (F.A.R.M.S.: 1993), Semester 4:138–39.

25. Spencer W. Kimball, *The Miracle of Forgiveness,* 131.

26. Spencer W. Kimball, in Conference Report, October 1978, 63–64.

27. Joseph F. Smith, *Gospel Doctrine* (Salt Lake City: Deseret Book, 1939), 266.

28. *History of the Church*, 2:71–72.

29. Russell M. Nelson, in Conference Report, April 1985, 13.

30. Ibid.

31. Dallin H. Oaks, *Ensign*, November 1993, 74.

32. M. Russell Ballard, *Ensign*, October 1987, 8.

33. Bruce R. McConkie, *Mormon Doctrine*, 771.

34. *Encyclopedia of Mormonism*, s.v. "Suicide," 3:1422.

35. *Encyclopedia of Mormonism*, 2:971.

36. Lynn A. Mickelsen, in Conference Report, October 1995, 106.

37. George Albert Smith, in Conference Report, October 1932, 24.

7

"Thou Shalt Not Commit Adultery"

JOHN G. SCOTT

*S*OME TIME AGO I SAT IN my home watching a national news magazine program. During the latter part of the program the commentator announced that part of the broadcast would be devoted to the topic of prostitution. What I witnessed after the commercial break left me completely astonished.

Initially, the program dealt with the unseemly side of this sin. Then the balance of the broadcast was devoted to articulate and well-conceived arguments, by participants, supporting the notion that prostitution should be legalized. One woman plainly stated that since she had the right to an abortion, she also ought to have the right to use her body in any way she wanted. The arguments were compelling and emotional. The news organization intervie-

---

John G. Scott is the director of the Beaumont, Texas, Institute of Religion and the co-editor of Riches of Eternity, Twelve Fundamental Doctrines from the Doctrine and Covenants *and* Riches of Faith. *He and his wife, Valene, are the parents of six children.*

wees included both men and women who participated regularly in the "world's oldest profession." The positive aspects of legalized prostitution were further elaborated on by brothel owners in Nevada, where in certain counties prostitution is legal.

I watched this program thinking to myself how amazing it is that Satan could so easily "creep into houses, and lead captive silly women laden with sins, led away with divers lusts" (2 Timothy 3:6). These women and men arguing for legalized prostitution had become captives of their own lusts. Unfortunately, this sad commentary seems to be a strong indication as to the direction in which our society is heading.

Fortunately the program also featured an interview with a member of The Church of Jesus Christ of Latter-day Saints. Senator Orrin Hatch offered a defense of morality and family in the face of this reckless expression of immorality. In his interview, Brother Hatch talked about the importance of the family unit, how the move to legalize prostitution would strike at the very foundations of family life and security, and how the very notion of prostitution was contrary to the commandments of God. The commentator appeared to mirror the world's reaction, for he grew agitated at Brother Hatch's comments and seemed to dismiss them as narrow-mindedness.

This interview, and in fact the entire broadcast, highlighted the fact that the Church and the world are heading in two opposite directions with regard to the seventh commandment. The world's moral compass has been sadly misdirected by the philosophies of lust, pride, and arrogance. At times there doesn't seem to be any way to head off the rising tide of immorality in the world. However, as thoughtful believers in Jesus Christ, we know that a stand must be taken and that we have a responsibility to be a light unto the world (see Matthew 5:14–16).

Specifically, this chapter will focus on three major areas relative to the seventh commandment, "Thou shalt not commit adultery" (Exodus 20:14). Discussion will first center on the eternal nature of this commandment and the fact that current societal changes have not altered God's direction to His children. Second, our focus will be directed to how this law protects the foundation of the family unit and the right of the child to have a mother and a father to guide them in the path of truth and righteousness. Third, we will explore the eternal nature of the punishments God has attached to the breaking of the seventh commandment.

ETERNAL LAW—ABSOLUTE TRUTH

The moral laws encompassed by the Ten Commandments are basic to much of civilization. These commandments form the basis of the United States Constitution as well as many of the laws that exist throughout that nation and the world.[1] Prohibitions against stealing, murder, adultery, and so on, are so common, it is reasonable to assert that the Ten Commandments form the basis of a collective understanding of what is morally right and wrong.

The seventh commandment is one of the giants among the comprehensive Ten Commandments. "Thou shalt not commit adultery" (Exodus 20:14) has been the basis of many legal statutes regarding moral activity within our nation and its communities since the establishment of the republic.[2] The founding fathers recognized a sense of the divine in the Ten Commandments, and this is why so many fundamental governing laws mirrored the philosophy found in the Decalogue.[3] These included many laws forbidding the practice of adultery and establishing severe criminal penalties for the breaking of this law.

Anyone who believes in God and has even a casual understanding of our nation's history cannot but acknowledge that our nation has been blessed by God. Father Lehi made a point of the importance of obedience in obtaining these blessings when he said: "Wherefore, I, Lehi, have obtained a promise, that inasmuch as those whom the Lord God shall bring out of the land of Jerusalem shall keep his commandments, they shall prosper upon the face of this land; and they shall be kept from all other nations, that they may possess this land unto themselves. And if it so be that they shall keep his commandments they shall be blessed upon the face of this land, and there shall be none to molest them, nor to take away the land of their inheritance; and they shall dwell safely forever." (2 Nephi 1:9.)

The Book of Mormon contains ample evidence that these blessings were confirmed upon the Nephite people when they were obedient, and they were revoked during their disobedience. This notion of divine approbation because of obedience to the commandments of God was a widely held belief among our fore-fathers.[4] Unfortunately, today many of the inhabitants of our nation are not aware of the importance of the Ten Command-ments, much less the importance of obedience to them. Because of this, the seventh commandment is thought of as a narrow-minded form of moral restriction. However logical this current trend of thought may appear to be, it is nevertheless wrong. The commandment to not commit adultery has its root in eternal law that has never become outdated.

This law, simply stated, is that there should be no sexual rela-tions of any kind before marriage and that a man and a woman are to practice complete fidelity after marriage. Any deviation from this is sin. This is the moral law that God expects each of His children to uphold. In speaking of this moral code, President Spencer W. Kimball stated:

> That the Church's stand on morality may be understood, we declare firmly and unalterably, it is not an outworn gar-ment, faded, old-fashioned, and threadbare. God is the same yesterday, today, and forever, and his covenants and doctrines are immutable; and when the sun grows cold and the stars no longer shine, the law of chastity will still be basic in God's world and in the Lord's church. Old values are upheld by the Church not because they are old, but rather because through the ages they have proved right. It will always be the rule.[5]

This thoughtful statement clearly points out that the admoni-tion to not commit adultery—in other words, to keep the law of chastity—is an eternal principle that does not change to meet the whims of society's perceived wants. This law governs not only our present stage of existence but also will be the norm throughout all eternity.

Even before the Decalogue was given (Exodus chapter 20) the law of chastity was in force. This law was given to Adam and Eve when they were in the Garden of Eden. The scripture states: "Therefore shall a man leave his father and his mother, and shall cleave unto his wife; and they shall be one flesh" (Moses 3:24). Clearly, Adam was to rely on, relate to, or be one with Eve, his wife. According to this admonition there was to be no room for anyone else.

We find further evidence for this law in the pre-Mosaic era of the great patriarchs. One example can be found in a story told about Jacob's son Joseph. While a slave in Egypt Joseph found himself in a very compromising situation because of the advances of the wife of Potiphar, his master. She wanted Joseph to have a sexual relationship with her even though she was married. Joseph's response to this woman is a telling one. He said: "How then can I do this great wickedness, and sin against God?" (Genesis 39:9.) From Joseph's comment we learn that he knew a moral code. He knew that to "lie" with Potiphar's wife would be a moral wrong. Joseph was aware that were he to act in an adulterous way this would offend God; it would break one of God's fundamental laws: Thou shalt not commit adultery.

Abinadi taught all of the Ten Commandments to the court of wicked King Noah (see Mosiah 13:22). From Abinadi's comments we learn that the Nephites were aware of the eternal law forbidding the practice of adultery. David Rolph Seely concurs that the Nephites had long understood this law:

The phrase "commit adultery" occurs six times outside Abinadi's quotation of the commandments and the passage in the Sermon on the Mount that Jesus teaches to the Nephites (3 Nephi 12:27–32). The English word *adultery* does not occur in the translation of the small plates at all. On the small plates the term for immorality is most often rendered "whoredoms." For example, Jacob spoke to the Nephites, "Wo unto them who commit whoredoms" (2 Nephi 9:36) and "For I, the Lord God, delight in the chastity of women. And whoredoms are an abomination before me" (Jacob 2:28; see also v. 33). Nephi warned latter-day readers "that they should not commit whoredoms" (2 Nephi 26:32). Whereas the term "commit whoredoms" covers a broad range of immorality, it often occurs in contexts suggesting it to be synonymous with adultery.[6]

Not only did the Nephites understand the injunction to not commit adultery, but the Savior himself taught this absolute and eternal truth to His disciples in the old world. In the Sermon on the Mount Jesus offered the higher law, which amplified the strong teachings found in the Mosaic code of truth. Jesus said: "Ye have heard that it was said by them of old time, Thou shalt not commit adultery: but I say unto you, That whosoever looketh on a woman to lust after her hath committed adultery with her already in his heart" (Matthew 5:27–28).

Clearly, the Savior taught the multitude gathered on the shores of Galilee a loftier interpretation of the seventh commandment. Jesus conveyed eternal truths in His sermon on the mount, and He meant for us to live these principles.

As part of the restoration of truth in the latter days, Jesus once again revealed through a prophet, Joseph Smith, "Thou shalt not commit adultery" (D&C 42:24). Emphasizing the truth that He taught in the Sermon on the Mount, Jesus said: "And verily I say unto you, as I have said before, he that looketh on a woman to lust after her, or if any shall commit adultery in their hearts, they shall not have the spirit, but shall deny the faith and shall fear" (D&C 63:16; see also D&C 42:23).

From these examples there emerges a clear pattern of the high priority that God has placed on the seventh commandment. This moral code is taught throughout the standard works, and it permeates the teachings of the prophets. The commandment to not commit adultery is an eternal law. This law will never be altered, abbreviated, or abdicated.

SEVENTH COMMANDMENT PROTECTS THE FAMILY UNIT

What happens to a family when one (or both) of the parents commits adultery? Many sad tales could be told of the heartache and the hours of bitter tears that follow the commission of this sin. Our modern society has become plagued with broken homes and hearts because of the violation of the seventh commandment.

Of particular sadness is the loss of confidence in and respect for the offending partner. Through the loss of this respect the ability of that person to influence his or her children for righteousness is greatly diminished.

The family is basic to God's divine plan of happiness for each individual. Through parenthood "we have been given the power to clothe the spirit progeny of God with physical bodies. In this way we become copartners with God in fulfilling his purpose of bringing his spirit children into mortality with a body."[7]

God fully intended that each parent should then teach his or her children the principles of the gospel: "And again, inasmuch as parents have children in Zion, or in any of her stakes which are organized, that teach them not to understand the doctrine of repentance, faith in Christ the Son of the living God, and of baptism and the gift of the Holy Ghost by the laying on of the hands, when eight years old, the sin be upon the heads of the parents" (D&C 68:25). And the Lord added: "And they shall also teach their children to pray, and to walk uprightly before the Lord" (D&C 68:28).

Good example, trust, and respect are essential ingredients in the teaching process the Lord has outlined for parents. Effectiveness in the teaching of gospel truth is severely limited when a child knows that a parent is not living the gospel. Alma taught his son Corianton the power of example in the teaching process. After Corianton had been involved in an immoral relationship Alma explained how this had hurt the work of the Lord: "Behold, O my son, how great iniquity ye brought upon the Zoramites; for when they saw your conduct they would not believe in my words" (Alma 39:11).

As with Corianton, our bad example can have a negative impact upon our family. Perhaps the most dramatic negative impact that adultery has on any family is the break-up of that family. Trust is an essential factor in marriage.[8] When trust is lost in marriage it is often extremely hard to recover. This loss of trust often leads couples to the divorce courts, and the family is blown apart. The destruction of the family has become a plague upon our society.

Naturally, the Lord and His prophets feel great concern about the integrity of the family unit. In the fall of 1995, the First Presidency and the Council of the Twelve Apostles announced a proclamation to the world. This proclamation made clear the Lord's feelings about the importance of the family. In part, the proclamation declared that "marriage between a man and a woman is ordained of God and that the family is central to the Creator's plan for the eternal destiny of his children." It continued:

> The first commandment that God gave to Adam and Eve pertained to their potential for parenthood as husband and wife. We declare that God's commandment for His children to multiply and replenish the earth remains in force. We further declare that God has commanded that the sacred powers of procreation are to be employed only between man and woman, lawfully wedded as husband and wife. . . .
>
> Children are entitled to birth within the bonds of matrimony, and to be reared by a father and a mother who honor marital vows with complete fidelity. Happiness in family life is most likely to be achieved when founded upon the teachings of the Lord Jesus Christ. . . .

In summation, the proclamation read:

> We warn that individuals who violate covenants of chastity, who abuse spouse or offspring, or who fail to fulfill family responsibilities will one day stand accountable before

God. Further, we warn that the disintegration of the family will bring upon the individuals, communities, and nations the calamities foretold by ancient and modern prophets.[9]

Clearly, the Lord is pleading with couples everywhere to forsake the evil of adultery. Equally clear is the implication that the failure to do so will eventually result in the demise of the family, the foundation for a stable society. Adultery quickly erodes this foundation through the confusion, breakup and turmoil it so often causes a family. The family is one of God's highest priorities; therefore, to break up a family becomes one of the greatest crimes anyone can commit. For this reason, God has simply said: "Thou shalt not commit adultery." Accepting this one commandment will go a long way to preserving the integrity of the family.

A PUNISHMENT AFFIXED TO THE BREAKING OF THIS COMMANDMENT

Anciently, the penalty for adultery was severe. The Mosaic law prescribed: "And the man that committeth adultery with another man's wife, even he that committeth adultery with his neighbour's wife, the adulterer and the adulteress shall surely be put to death" (Leviticus 20:10). The seriousness of this penalty mirrors the seriousness with which God views the breaking of the commandment.

Through Jesus' ministry to the people, a different version of punishment was instituted. When an adulterous woman is brought to Jesus, we learn of the road to repentance: "And the scribes and Pharisees brought unto him [Jesus] a woman taken in adultery; and when they had set her in the midst, they say unto him, Master, this woman was taken in adultery, in the very act. Now Moses in the law commanded us, that such should be stoned: but what sayest thou?" (John 8:3–5.)

Clearly those gathered were trying to pit the Savior against the law of Moses, which would discredit His own teachings that the law of Moses had been fulfilled in Him. However, being very patient, the Savior reminded those gathered that they were not without sin.

After the crowd had melted away, the Savior said to the woman: "Woman, where are those thine accusers? hath no man condemned thee? She said, No man, Lord. And Jesus said unto her, Neither do I condemn thee: go, and sin no more." (John 8:10–11.)

Some have believed that the woman was let off too easy for this serious sin. In fact, however, she was unforgiven at this point. But her sin had been confessed in a very public way. The Master's injunction to her to "go, and sin no more" was the first step down a long road which would eventually lead to complete forgiveness and rehabilitation. The woman was repentant, her sins had been confessed, and her priesthood authority had determined the course of her repentance. The law had been fulfilled.

In the restored Church the Lord has counseled: "and he that committeth adultery, and repenteth not, shall be cast out" (D&C 42:24). Thus the adulterer may suffer excommunication or disfellowshipment from the Church. If he is truly repentant, however, he can find forgiveness and be reinstated.

> Because adultery or fornication breaks baptismal covenants and temple vows and may involve other members of the Church, penitent offenders are to confess the sin to their bishop or other Church authority, who may convene a disciplinary council. After prayerful deliberation, the council may excommunicate or disfellowship an adulterer, or implement some type of probation to help the offender repent. The excommunication of an adulterous priesthood leader is almost certain. A disciplinary council usually requires the adulterer to seek forgiveness from the betrayed spouse and from anyone drawn into the sin. By demonstrating an abhorrence for past sin and a commitment to righteousness, the repentant adulterer may, after an adequate period of probation, become fully reconciled to Christ, rebaptized, and reinstated in the Church and find forgiveness from God (D&C 58:47–48).[10]

This punishment of being severed from the Church fits the enormity of the crime. Because adultery is so frequently accepted in the world, we sometimes forget its serious nature. In counseling a wayward Corianton as regards the seriousness of breaking the law of chastity Alma suggested: "Know ye not, my son, that these things are an abomination in the sight of the Lord; yea, most abominable above all sins save it be the shedding of innocent blood or denying the Holy Ghost?" (Alma 39:5.) Elder Spencer W. Kimball gave an even plainer rendering when he said: "The Lord apparently rates adultery close to premeditated murder."[11]

While there is serious consequence for breaking this commandment, excommunication or disfellowshipment can begin the healing process for the one who has committed the sin. Through loving and caring priesthood leaders the offender may be brought back into full fellowship with the Church once the repentance process has been completed. Thus the offender is helped through the process of repentance and is strengthened in his or her resolve to do what is right. While this process is not easy because of the serious nature of the sin, with full repentance all former blessings may be regained by the offender, including self-respect and the trust of others.

The unrepentant adulterer will inherit the lowest kingdom of glory, the telestial kingdom, for this is the dwelling place for those who are "liars, and sorcerers, and adulterers, and whoremongers, and whosoever loves and makes a lie" (D&C 76:103). This scripture makes clear the eternal punishments and consequences associated with the breaking of the seventh commandment. These punishments are specific and relatively severe, not because God is vindictive but because the laws concerned are eternal and never-changing. When our universe ceases to exist and we have progressed far beyond this realm in our eternal journey, the injunction to not commit adultery will still be in force among all of God's children and so will the consequences for disobedience.

CONCLUSION

The seventh commandment is short, only five words long. The simplicity of the commandment may reflect its strength. In a straightforward way God has commanded us to stay away from something very specific—the act of being sexually immoral, the act of adultery. And while society may dash itself to pieces against this eternal bedrock, that will not alter this unchangeable law.

The world needs a healthy dose of moral character. Everyone in society would do well to take careful note of the seventh commandment. If the commandment to not commit adultery were taken as seriously as God meant it to be, society would enjoy greater peace, greater love and trust, and a greater sense of divine approbation.

God loves His children and wants them to be happy. It is for this reason that He gave the Ten Commandments in the first place. Happiness comes in obeying eternal laws. As we avoid adultery, our families will be stronger and the relationships between spouses will be healthier. Through obedience to this commandment we can rest assured that we will never have to worry about the consequences associated with disobeying the seventh commandment. In short, obedience to the seventh commandment brings peace, love, and family unity. By obedience to this law we will also come closer to God.

In Joseph Smith's words:

If you wish to go where God is, you must be like God, or possess the principles which God possesses, for if we are not drawing towards God in principle, we are going from Him and drawing towards the devil. Yes, I am standing in the midst of all kinds of people.

Search your hearts, and see if you are like God. I have searched mine, and feel to repent of all my sins.

We have thieves among us, adulterers, liars, hypocrites. If God should speak from heaven, he would command you not to steal, not to commit adultery, not to covet, nor deceive, but be faithful over a few things. As far as we degenerate from God, we descend to the devil and lose knowledge, and without knowledge we cannot be saved, and while our hearts are filled with evil, and we are studying evil, there is no room in our hearts for good, or studying good.[12]

God wants us to become like Him. Only through the wise use of our agency and obedience to the commandments of God can we develop the nature of God and fully become as He is. May there always be room in our hearts for good, even the goodness of practicing right principles.

Notes

1. For a brief treatment on the view of The Church of Jesus Christ of Latter-day Saints on the United States Constitution see *Encyclopedia of Mormonism,* s.v. "Constitution of the United States of America," 1:317–19.

2. For a greater understanding of the relationship between the eternal laws of God and the establishment of the United States of America see Ezra Taft Benson, *The Teachings of Ezra Taft Benson* (Salt Lake City: Bookcraft, 1988), 612–25; hereafter *Teachings.*

3. For a brief explanation concerning the word *Decalogue* see David P. Wright, "Revelations in the Wilderness of Sinai" in *Studies in Scripture, Vol. 3: Genesis to 2 Samuel,* ed. Kent P. Jackson and Robert L. Millet (Salt Lake City: Deseret Book, 1989), 125.

4. *Teachings,* 621.

5. Spencer W. Kimball, *Ensign,* November 1980, 96.

6. David Roth Seely, "The Ten Commandments in the Book of Mormon," in *Doctrines of the Book of Mormon, the 1991 Sperry Symposium* (Salt Lake City: Deseret Book, 1992), 173.

7. John G. Scott, "The Purpose of Mortality," in *Riches of Eternity,* ed. John K. Challis, John G. Scott (Salt Lake City: Aspen Books, 1993), 66.

8. See Stephen R. Covey and Truman G. Madsen, *Marriage and Family: Gospel Insights* (Salt Lake City: Bookcraft, 1983), 71.

9. "The Family, A Proclamation To The World," *Ensign,* November 1995, 102.

10. *Encyclopedia of Mormonism,* s.v. "Adultery," 1:21.

11. Spencer W. Kimball, *The Miracle of Forgiveness* (Salt Lake City: Bookcraft, 1969), 62.

12. Joseph Smith, *Teachings of the Prophet Joseph Smith*, comp. Joseph Fielding Smith (Salt Lake City: Deseret Book, 1977), 216–17.

8

"Thou Shalt Not Steal"

JOHN K. CHALLIS

A STUDENT SEEKING HELP for a sacrament meeting talk asked me, "What am I going to say in an *entire* talk about the eighth commandment—'Thou shalt not steal'?" (Exodus 20:15.) "After all, isn't it spoken in plain enough terms—everyone understands that if it's not yours you don't take it." Well, in our ensuing discussion I was able to illustrate for him that there is indeed much more to this commandment and its relevancy today. The discussion that follows will present a few of the aspects he and I discussed about stealing and its effect on the human condition—both temporally and spiritually.

First, we will consider a present trend in our culture to trivialize, and thus trifle with, God's commands. Second, we will discuss the relationship between the doctrinal dimension of unity

John K. Challis is the director of the Afton Institute of Religion in Afton, Wyoming and the co-editor of Riches of Eternity, Twelve Fundamental Doctrines from the Doctrine and Covenants *and* Riches of Faith. *He and his wife, Julie, are the parents of five daughters.*

and stealing. Finally, we will focus our attention on the soul-crippling nature of dishonesty, emphasizing the interrelatedness of clean hands and pure hearts (see Psalm 24:3–5).

SOME SPECIFIC TEACHINGS ABOUT STEALING

The Ten Commandments are the foundational principles of righteousness, and they deal with all aspects of human moral and spiritual behavior. After seven of these divine edicts had been given to Moses on Sinai (see Exodus 20), the Lord declared, "Thou shalt not steal" (v. 15). Thus the eighth commandment became of force to ancient Israel, and it continues to be binding upon the world today. President Spencer W. Kimball, citing modern revelation, taught: "In public office and private lives, the word of the Lord thunders: 'Thou shalt not steal. . . . nor do anything like unto it' (D&C 59:6). . . . To all thieveries and dishonest acts, the Lord says, 'Thou shalt not steal.' Four short common words He used."[1]

Clearly, the eighth commandment is a God-given law and the passage of time has not lessened its efficacy. It is the Lord's law concerning moral and spiritual honesty, and as it relates to mortality it is a measurement of our actions toward our neighbors—and their property. Even on its most superficial level, the eighth commandment is justifiable and of merit, for it exposes to view (either immediately, or over time) a person's real honesty (think of the Apostle John's appraisal of Judas, John 13:26–27), mirroring the soul's condition. As a matter of fact, it is the forthright simplicity of the eighth commandment that brings validity to its language concerning stealing. It is a simple test: if something is stolen, it is stolen, and someone is responsible. "Nothing just walks away," my mother once taught me concerning this very commandment.

THE SERIOUSNESS OF TRIFLING WITH GOD'S EIGHTH COMMANDMENT

It goes almost without saying, at least to a person of faith, that any word spoken by Jehovah through His servants on earth, His mouthpieces, is sacred. Nevertheless it appears that many in today's world, either through choice or ignorance, have lost sight of this doctrinal reality. Early in our dispensation, for example, the Lord taught His servant Oliver Cowdery through His spokesman Joseph Smith to "[t]rifle not with sacred things" (D&C 6:12). The Lord had already revealed to Oliver in this same communication, that things of sacredness "cometh from above" (6:10). It follows that this applies to our day as well. We should not trifle with sacred things which come from above, not the least of which is the commandment "Thou shalt not steal."

The prophet Joseph made this crystal clear by teaching: "We believe that God condescended to speak from the heavens and declare His will concerning the human family, to give them just and holy laws, to regulate their conduct, and guide them in a direct way. . . . For these reasons, If we have direct revelations given us from heaven, surely those revelations were never given to be trifled with."[2]

The Lord also desires that all in mortality be happy and live free from the bondage of sin. Every commandment, the Prophet Joseph taught, is "calculated in its nature to promote that happiness which he has designed, and . . . end in the greatest amount of good and glory" for those who keep His commandments.[3] There are those today who do not understand that spiritual freedom is a companion to keeping the commandments (see John 8:32). These individuals frequently employ a much used sleight-of-hand trick that I have labeled "semantic swapping." For example, in the case of the eighth commandment, the phrase "previously owned" is sometimes swapped for the term "used" in the attempt to sell a second-hand car. Is this an honest attempt to have the consumer feel better about a purchase? One wonders.

Such semantic swapping is closely akin to the practice of rationalization. The book *The Synonym Finder* gives the first synonym for rationalize as "intellectualize." This is followed by "explain away," and finally, "to make acceptable."[4] Such rationalization may be viewed as the world's[5] attempt to soften a command of the Lord—to explain it away, even make it more pleasing and acceptable. Clearly this is a problem prevalent in our society when it comes to honesty, theft, stealing, and the like. Elder Dallin H. Oaks has taught with wry truthfulness, "Not all stealing is at gunpoint or by dark of night. Some theft is by deception, where the thief manipulates the confidence of the victim."[6]

Is It Possible to Make a Commandment More "Acceptable"?

"Thou shalt not command," a headline shouted above a commentary piece published in a popular national magazine. The article began with these eight words: "These are dark days for the Ten Commandments." It seemed to be a herald, serving unreserved notice that many feel the Ten Commandments are obsolete. The article stated: "It's not just that people go around breaking them all the time (nothing new there), but that so few of us seem able to remember what these oft-broken rules actually say."

Now, to someone who reveres the word of God, such talk is both alarming and thought-provoking. For example, one may wonder, do people really go around breaking the Ten Commandments *all the time*? Of course not! It may be true that they are "oft-broken," but another question arises: What is the implication behind the semantic swapping of the term "rules" for "commandments"? It could be argued that this is an interjection of the view of many, which goes something like this: "It's much easier to violate or ignore a commandment of God if we have 'diluted it down' to rule status."

It seems apparent from reading this article that we must have concern about our society's devaluation of the Ten Commandments—in our case "thou shalt not steal." However, when the article further states "surely it is time to spruce up these 3,000-

year-old Commandments and render them memorable and pleasing,"[7] one wonders. Furthermore, what of this desire to make a commandment more "pleasing"? The Prophet Alma comes to mind. This great servant was very "grieved for the iniquity of his people," he knew of the various indictments against them, and then saw "that the hearts of the people began to wax hard, and that they began to be *offended because of the strictness of the word*" (Alma 35:15, emphasis added).

The word does appear strict to those who, by choice, will not live by it. Such rebellious souls offend the Holy Spirit and, thus left to themselves, see the word as a stifling, even burdensome thing. As a result, they may never come to understand, as do those who live by it, that true freedom comes from conforming oneself to the law and living by it. Then it is possible for the Spirit to reside with this lawful (i.e., full of the law) person and grant freedom. For, "where the Spirit of the Lord is, there is liberty" (2 Corinthians 3:17). Additionally, we know that the wicked are easily offended as the word also tends to strike at the chords of the soul's guilt (see 2 Nephi 1:26; 33:5; and 1 Nephi 16:1–3). One fruit of unrighteous offense is a need to reduce feelings of guilt by adding water to their medicine of accountability. This watering-down has taken shape in a trend aimed at rendering the Ten Commandments more "pleasing." This would change the eighth commandment, for example, from "thou shalt not steal," to, "thou shalt not steal, but creative work on your tax return is OK." Of course, this keeps the "bossy language" of the original commandment, while adding a modern loophole.[8]

What kind of individual, it could be asked, would seek to change a commandment? Perhaps someone needing to feel better about his behavior. Consider President David O. McKay's statement that "the first condition of happiness is a clear conscience."[9] When the need to trivialize a commandment of God is factored in, then this teaching from President McKay takes on added meaning. Trivializing a commandment of God is merely a vain attempt to find happiness in sin. It illustrates a mortal approach to maneuver around one's conscience by treating lightly the thing pricking it. For example if the divine edict "Thou shalt not steal" can be passed off as nothing, it becomes much easier to shed off any guilt that accompanies not keeping it. President James E. Faust has declared, "Many modern professors of human behavior advocate as a cure to an afflicted conscience that we simply ignore the unwanted messages. They suggest that we change the standard to fit the circumstances so that there is no longer a conflict, thus easing the conscience. The followers of the divine Christ cannot subscribe to this evil and perverse philosophy with impunity. For the troubled conscience in conflict with right and wrong, the only permanent help is to change the behavior and follow a repentant path."[10]

"THOU SHALT NOT STEAL" AND THE DOCTRINE OF UNITY

When the Lord Jehovah first appeared to Moses, and began training this prophet at the "burning bush," He underscored the sacred nature of entering into the divine presence by saying, "Draw not nigh hither: put off thy shoes from off thy feet, for the place whereon thou standest is holy ground" (Exodus 3:5). This place was made holy because the Lord Jehovah was literally there. And His admonition to Moses concerning his shoes is of great importance. It is emblematic in many ways. Here we will consider only two.

First, Moses' shoes were a primary connection between his body and the world, quite literally, as in "where the rubber meets the road." As Moses removed his shoes, he removed the barrier of the world. There was nothing now separating Moses from the mountain's holy ground—the same ground—which Jehovah stood upon also. Thus the Lord had removed a barrier from Moses, creating the possibility of heightened "oneness" or unity. Second, Moses' shoes (i.e., the world) being literally and significantly absent, betoken in a sublime and dignified manner that things worldly are not allowed in God's presence. "Remove the world from you," the Lord is symbolically teaching, "for where I am, things of the world cannot come." Additionally, removing the world from us, and placing behind us obsessions with acquiring the tokens of the world (wealth, jewels, and the toys of our modern age) increases our power to become one with the Lord. "I say into you, be one; and if ye are not one ye are not mine" (D&C 38:27; see also John 17: 14–21).

These teachings, punctuated in Exodus 3:5, further emphasize the sacred seriousness of any interview with Deity. *Any* words spoken by the Lord intimate the reality of the Lord's personal involvement in our affairs. They illustrate His desire to teach by example that unity with Him is attainable—and that He will do His part. It cannot be overstated that Jehovah personally interacted with Moses, whether in this first instance or at other times (see Moses 1; Exodus 24:9–12; 33:11). Furthermore, when Jehovah instructed Moses to say to the people: "Thou shalt not steal" (see Exodus 20:15; Moses 1) it was not casual "how is the weather" chatter, but solemn and reflective heavenly counsel. Counsel given, with the creation of greater unity and power among His people at its center. The Prophet Joseph understood this, for he once stated in simple beauty, "Unity is power."[11] Truly, that which comes from above is sacred and carries with it nothing that is trivial. Nothing given us from the Lord is open to change (D&C 1:38), much less to rationalization or dilution through the swapping—or substitution of terms—in the language of a commandment. There is power in such words, power coming as blessings; and, in the case of the eighth commandment, the power of unity that honesty and trust foster. Moses understood this, and most assuredly witnessed in the wandering children of Israel the divisive results of dishonesty. Joseph Smith, in a parallel manner, was taught this principle through observation and revelation.

THE SAINTS "IN THE OHIO" AND THE EFFECTS OF HONESTY

Joseph Smith was the recipient of many revelations and divine communications. He was given first-hand the knowledge and right to speak concerning that which comes from above. "It is a great thing," Joseph taught, "to inquire at the hands of God, or to come into His presence; and we feel fearful to approach Him on subjects that are of little or no consequence."[12] This understanding would eventually lead him to say that, "I want you to know that God, in the last days . . . is not trifling with you or me."[13]

Certainly Joseph made the statement above knowing full well the weight of these words: "This generation shall have my word through you" (D&C 5:10). Such knowledge, it appears, came to Joseph during—or following—extreme experiences the Lord had caused His servant to pass through. Two of these extremities illustrate well that much of the Lord's word came not with ease and convenience, but with inconvenience. First, Joseph was coun-seled of the Lord to leave the comforting hearth and home of New York—his native country—and "go to the Ohio" to receive God's law (D&C 38:32). And, once in the Ohio, the word of law was given. It stated in part, "Thou shalt not steal; and he that stealeth and will not repent shall be cast out" (D&C 42:20).

Similarly, after slogging hundreds of miles on foot, Joseph received the law of God for the Saints in the wilderness of Mis-souri. Amid windowless log huts, dirt floors, and skin-clad ruffi-ans, Joseph a second time received the words of law and com-mandment. This divine communication, given for those in Zion, had the sacred intent of assisting these Saints to remain unspotted from the world. It included the familiar language of the eighth commandment, "Thou shalt not steal," and added "nor do any-thing like unto it" (D&C 59:6). The words immediately preced-ing this edict state, "Thou shalt love thy neighbor as thyself" (v. 6). Certainly, any commandment founded on the principle of love, having a person and his neighbor as key players, will bear the fruit of increased unity—not to mention the fruitfulness of "being one" and belonging to the Lord (see D&C 38:27).

Perhaps the following example will serve well to illustrate the interrelationship of honest actions and unity. When the Prophet Joseph arrived in the Ohio, he found the newly converted Saints striving to do the will of the Lord based on their limited gospel understanding. Being young in the Church, they engaged in certain practices not approved of the Lord through His mouthpiece. In speaking of these novice Saints and their activities, Joseph Smith labeled their behavior as "strange notions and false spirits."[14]

One such "strange notion" encountered by the Prophet Joseph was a social experiment of sharing things in common. The central philosophy of this society could best be described as, "what's yours is mine." The society had at its basis a limited number of people living in a self-sufficient and small community. It was primarily a practice found in the Northeastern United States, and the "communities could be religious or secular."[15]

A group of well-meaning Saints had established a community of this nature on the Isaac Morley farm, and were known as the "Family." They considered what belonged to one as belonging to any in the society, and John Whitmer (the Prophet's first emissary to the Ohio), wrote, "therefore they would take each others clothes and other property and use it without leave: which brought on confusion and disappointment."[16] Levi Hancock, a new convert to the Latter-day Saints, was taken to the Morley farm by a fellow Saint, Harvey Redfield, and wrote of his experience: "Isaac Morley was a cooper by trade and one of the most honest patient men I have ever seen. The company he maintained looked large enough to bring on a famine. I do not know if they [the family] lived on him all the time or not. While I was in the room at 'Father Morley's,' as we called him, Heman Bassett came to me and took my watch out of my pocket and walked off as though it was his. I thought he would bring it back soon but was disappointed as he sold it. I asked him what he meant by selling my watch. 'Oh,' said he, 'I thought it was all in the family.' I told him I did not like such family doings and I would not bear it."[17] This experience of Brother Hancock's illustrates that such practices were destined to destroy unity. That without clearly defined laws and obligations, feelings would run high, and therefore the experiment was "fast going to destruction," in John Whitmer's estimation.[18]

Brother Hancock's experience also highlights why additional wisdom and insight was sent to Joseph Smith from heaven. The word of the Lord was given to correct many false teachings, beliefs, and the "strange notions" evidenced in Ohio. Nevertheless this new insight was given to the Prophet (building upon the already received "law" known as Section 42), without "noise or physical manifestations," Orson Pratt recalled. That "Joseph was as calm as the morning sun . . . [and] his face was exceedingly white,"[19] when he received the following divine instruction: "And let every man deal honestly, and be alike among this people, and receive alike, that ye may be one, even as I have commanded you" (D&C 51:9).

It appears that the Lord wanted the Saints to understand that principles of unity were founded not only on good intentions but also on principles of honest conduct. If one distrusts another, especially when belonging to the same faith or society, surely unity cannot exist. This underscores further the importance of one of the Lord's foundational teachings, "If ye are not one ye are not mine" (D&C 38:27).

PSALM 24 AND "THOU SHALT NOT STEAL"

Inspiration and the spirit of prophecy were poured out upon those psalmists who, over the centuries, composed the sacred hymns in the book of Psalms. It originated in the days of King David and his son Solomon and served as ancient Israel's hymnal. "The Hebrew title is *Tehillin,* meaning 'praises.' . . . It is the Old Testament book most often quoted in the New Testament." And, most important of all, "Jesus referred to the Psalms more often than any other Old Testament book."[20] Indeed, the acuteness of the Lord's feelings toward the Psalms is demonstrated in His final act with the eleven remaining Apostles. The Lord would soon face Gethsemane, false trials and mockery, and then Golgotha— alone. But before meeting these challenges, He took a moment and in a simple yet profound act led the eleven in a hymn. Both Matthew and Mark retell it thus: "And when they had sung an hymn, they went out into the mount of Olives" (Matthew 26:30; Mark 14:26). Of all the things the Lord could have said or done, He chose a hymn (most assuredly a psalm) for His eleven disciples' final memory prior to the mighty working of the Atonement.

Therefore, without equivocation, a phrase from Psalm 24 is used here to reinforce the consequences related to the Lord's commandment of "Thou shalt not steal" (Exodus 20:15). The phrase is a common one: "He that hath clean hands, and a pure heart" (Psalm 24:4). In the following section we will consider the relationship between having clean hands and stealing.

HE THAT HATH CLEAN HANDS

In the thirteenth chapter of Romans, the Apostle Paul has eloquently affirmed:

> Owe no man any thing, but to love one another: for he that loveth another hath fulfilled the law.
>
> For this . . . thou shalt not steal . . . and if there be any other commandment, it is briefly comprehended in this saying, namely, Thou shalt love thy neighbor as thyself.
>
> Love worketh no ill to his neighbor . . . , The night is far spent, the day is at hand: Let us therefore cast off the works of darkness, and let us put on the armour of light.
>
> Let us walk honestly, as in the day. (Romans 13:8–13.)

In this passage Paul speaks plainly. He explains that people who do not love their neighbor will "work ill to his neighbor." That such people will participate in "works of darkness" and will not fulfill the law, because their dishonest actions demonstrate that they love themselves far more than anyone else. Paul here makes reference to the Lord's teaching that the first great commandment is to "love the Lord thy God, and the second is like unto it, Thou shalt love thy neighbor as thyself. On these two commandments hang all the law and the prophets." (Matthew 22:36–40.) Certainly an individual who treats any neighbor badly through a selfish work of darkness, such as stealing, can be said to have unclean hands.

In another setting, the Lord also used powerful imagery in illustrating His feelings toward one who would be a thief. He stated: "Verily, verily, I say unto you, he that entereth not by the door into the sheepfold, but climbeth up some other way, the same is a thief and a robber" (John 10:1). Are there any among us who lie awake at night (in the darkness), fearing that some stranger will break in and take their possessions? I think there are far too many. One who comes into a home (or office) by the door has used an honest and upfront entry, and of such we are rarely afraid. However, one who comes in by "some other way" (10:1) most assuredly is a thief or robber. For the "thief cometh not, but for to steal, and to kill, and to destroy," the Lord continued, and added, "I am come that they might have life, and that they might have it more abundantly" (John 10:10). A thief, the Lord seems to tell us, appears as one who is the direct opposite of "the way, the truth, and the life" (John 14:6). One employing his hand to steal walks in dishonesty, as in the night (the direct opposite of Romans 13:13), and will always seek some other way . And he is not only untrue, but unclean as well.

Elder Mark E. Petersen did not pull any punches when he said of this very concept, "Do we understand the gravity of the sin of dishonesty? It is not only unchristian, it is anti-Christian . . . it is anti-Christ! Whether it be lying, or cheating, or robbery or deception; whether it is in the home, in business, in sports, or in the classroom; dishonesty is completely foreign to the teachings of Jesus."[21] Therefore, when it comes to stealing, the Lord has made it clear—you do not take anything from another that does not belong to you or that has not been freely given to you. Period!

If you do steal from another, your hands are unclean because you have treated lightly the eighth commandment and have openly mocked the first and second great commandments. The commandment, "Thou shalt not steal," is based on eternal principles of honesty, integrity, and trust. And these principles just simply do not go out of fashion with God. It will never be the "thing to do," in God's eyes, to take from anyone their money or their house, their peace, jewelry, lawn edger, wife, husband, honesty, reputation, children, stereo, self-worth, or their trust.

A truly honest Latter-day Saint will love God and his neighbor as himself. He will lose all desire to hurt or make afraid a fellow member of the human family and he will become more like Christ. Teaching of this powerful truth, John proclaimed, "There is no fear in love; but perfect love casteth out fear" (1 John 4:18).

This sounds like charity to me. Mormon taught that "charity is the pure love of Christ" (Moroni 7:47), therefore one who is like Christ (think of Elder Petersen's comments above) would never take, but will give, always give. And the fruit of this behavior is becoming a just person who shall surely live. Consider Ezekiel 18: 5, 7-9: "But if a man be just, and do that which is lawful and right . . . and hath not oppressed any, but hath restored to the debtor his pledge, hath spoiled none by violence, hath given his bread to the hungry, and hath covered the naked with a garment. He that hath not given forth upon usury, neither hath taken any increase, *that hath withdrawn his hand from iniquity,* hath executed true judgment between man and man, hath walked in my statutes, and hath kept my judgments, to deal truly; he is just, he shall surely live, saith the Lord God." (Emphasis added.)

Only one of the Lord's anointed can say it that plainly. If a person wants to keep his hands clean and live (meaning eternal life), he will "withdraw his hand from iniquity," he will also "do that which is lawful and right," and will, as a result, "deal truly" with his neighbor.

One who has kept his hands clean from stealing, robbing, fraud, and the like, will find he has saved himself from the spiritually lethal consequences of this sin. President Spencer W. Kimball taught: "It is for us to keep our hearts and minds pure, as well as our actions. 'Thou shalt not steal,' the Lord said in Sinai (Exodus 20:15). Thus it is for us to be honest in every way. We must be generous, the very opposite of selfishness."[22] And in a similar manner, Elder George Albert Smith addressed the fate of those with unclean hands as a result of dishonesty. He said: "I want to say to you that the punishment that is meted out to those who are dishonest in our day, when they are apprehended and hauled before the courts of the land and punished for their crimes, is insignificant when compared with the spiritual punishment that befalls us when we transgress the law of honesty and violate the commandment of God."[23]

And finally, Elder Mark E. Petersen taught that honesty as a virtue is essential if one wants to obtain the celestial realms. Ponder these words of apostolic counsel: "We do not believe in honesty merely as matter of policy. It is far more important than that. Honesty is a principle of salvation in the kingdom of God. Without it there can be no salvation . . . As we cannot advance in the kingdom of heaven without a resurrection, so we cannot move into celestial realms without honesty."[24]

In summary, we in mortality do various things with our hands. We eat and work with them, and we also take the sacrament, sustain our leaders, and enter into covenants with our hands. Thus the Lord has rightfully warned, "Wherefore, let every man beware lest he do that which is not in truth and righteousness before me" (D&C 50:9). We should rightfully "beware" lest our hands become unclean and we lose our reward.

HE THAT HATH A PURE HEART

After discussing the outward, more visible aspect of stealing and its relation to having clean hands, we now turn to the inner, sometimes more easily concealed, aspect of stealing and its relation to the heart. To illustrate, let's begin with a question: Why is it so important to have a pure heart?

"Unto the pure all things are pure" stated Paul to Titus, "but unto them that are defiled and unbelieving is nothing pure; but even their mind and conscience is defiled" (Titus 1:15). Certainly one who is dishonest and a thief can be classified as impure—even defiled in his heart. As a spiritual symbol, the heart, which is the "inner man" (see Ephesians 3:16–17), is the center of creation for a person's actions. And the heart is nearly always linked scripturally with one's mind or thoughts. Consider the Lord's counsel to Oliver Cowdery that "there is none else save God that knowest thy thoughts and the intents of thy heart" (D&C 6:16). Therefore, it is important to have a pure heart, because it guarantees that our actions will also be pure. "Thought is the father of an act," Elder Harold B. Lee said. "The thief did not steal except he first coveted that which was his neighbor's."[25]

David emphasized the doctrinal relationship between the thoughts, heart, and actions of the wicked. "Hide from me the secret counsel of the wicked," he begins, for "they encourage themselves in an evil matter: they commune of laying snares privily; they say, Who shall see them? They search out iniquities; they accomplish a diligent search; both the *inward thought* of every one of them, and the heart, is deep." (Psalm 64: 2, 5–6, emphasis added.) Truly the heart "is deep," for it is capable of righteousness unto exaltation or of unrighteousness unto damnation. What is the effect of stealing on the heart and soul? President Spencer W. Kimball stated with prophetic emphasis, "The theft of pennies or dollars or commodities may impoverish little the one from whom the goods are taken, but it is a shrivelling, dwarfing process to the one who steals."[26]

When a person violates a commandment of God, it is not always easy to quell the feelings of guilt nor soothe the conscience. The "guilty taketh the truth to be hard, for it cutteth them to the very center" (1 Nephi 16:2). Therefore, many would salve their wounds through rationalization. They seek to lessen a strict adherence to the commandment of "Thou shalt not steal" by swapping "softer" more "pleasing" terms for the word *steal*. Such word substitution is an attempt to soften blows aimed at troubled consciences and diminish the effects dishonesty has on hearts and souls. But God has said of the wicked, "I know their works and their thoughts" (Isaiah 66:18). What follows illustrates the sweeping effect this form of rationalization has had on our world.

A SIN BY ANY OTHER NAME

The word *steal*, as used in the Bible, is the English translation of both a Hebrew and a Greek word. The Hebrew word is *ganab*, meaning "to thieve." This word *ganab* can also appear in English as "to deceive," to "secretly bring," or lastly "to steal away." Nevertheless, there was just one word for that open act of dishonesty—stealing—in the Hebrew scriptures (the Old Testament).

Similarly, the word *steal* is the English word used to translate the Greek term *klepto* in the New Testament. It means simply "to filch," and, unlike Hebrew (where there are two or three levels of meaning), the Greek scriptures (the New Testament) employ only one term, *klepto*, for the dishonest act of stealing.

In today's English, however, the term *steal* may be supplanted by roughly 128 synonymous words or phrases! The analogy is obvious. To Hebrew or Greek people in biblical times, if you stole something you were guilty of stealing. But, to English-speaking people today, there are at least 128 available options to down-play the fact that one has indeed stolen something. That means there are 128 ways to conceal, shade, or make one's dishonesty appear—well, more honest. This results in dishonest actions appearing more acceptable to the world, and the creation of a multitude of levels of dishonesty. Certainly if someone "purloins" an article from another, it doesn't sound as dark-a-deed as, say, "swindle." Likewise, "misappropriation" seems more like sloppy management than its alternative—"embezzlement."

CONCLUSION

Having a clean heart literally makes one free from sin and its cumbersome lifestyle. If we have a pure heart, we have no need to ever rationalize our behavior or to seek ways to dilute the strength that guilt wields on our conscience. Brigham Young once said, "simple truth . . . honesty, uprightness, justice, mercy, love, kindness, do good to all and evil to none, how easy it is to live by such principles! A thousand times easier than to practice deception."[27]

It is just as relevant today, as ever before, to obey the eighth commandment, "Thou shalt not steal." Upholding and obeying this commandment brings spiritual safety and peace to the soul. This commandment makes detecting the wicked among us a much easier process. If all on the earth were to keep this commandment, the love of God would fill our hearts, which would lead to safety; and this because we would not be in fear of anyone taking anything from us. Though one may rationalize all he wants about his thievish ways, and claim he has "clean hands, and a pure heart" (Psalm 24:4), the Lord will know differently. "For the word of God . . . is a discerner of the thoughts and intents of the heart" (Hebrews 4:12).

Elder John Taylor taught, "We may deceive one another, and, in some circumstances, as counterfeit coin passes for that which is considered true and valuable among men. But God searches the hearts and tries the reins of the children of men. He knows our thoughts and comprehends our desires and feelings; he knows our acts and the motives which prompt us to perform them. He is acquainted with all the doings and operations of the human family, and all the secret thoughts and acts of the children of men are open and naked before him, and for them he will bring them to judgment."[28]

Thus, building upon President Taylor's teachings, we should never take lightly those things we have received from above. Why? Because they carry with them eternal ramifications. Therefore we should take seriously every word that has proceeded from the mouth of the Lord to us in this world. We have been counseled very plainly to "trifle not with sacred things" (D&C 6:12), and one of these sacred things most assuredly is the eighth commandment. Obeying it will help us find spiritual peace and safety, and give us the blessing of clean hands and pure hearts. And those who know us will hail us as pure and clean. Others likewise will know through observation that we are people of honesty and integrity. Elder O. Leslie Stone said: "I like to think of reputation as a window, clearly exhibiting the integrity of one's soul. It is through this integrity of thought and integrity of conduct that we become pure and holy before the Lord. It is in this state that we can be most effective in serving our fellowmen."[29]

Notes

1. Spencer W. Kimball, *Ensign*, November 1976, 6.

2. Joseph Smith, *Teachings of the Prophet Joseph Smith*, comp. Joseph Fielding Smith (Salt Lake City: Deseret Book, 1977), 53–54. Hereafter cited as *TPJS*.

3. *TPJS*, 256.

4. Jeremy Irving Rodale, *The Synonym Finder* (Emmaus, PA: Rodale Press, 1978), 988. This last synonymous phrase "to make acceptable" provides a clear example of rationalization by semantic swapping. This is illustrated by citing a popular phrase proclaimed by many today: "Why can't you just accept us."

5. The phrase "of the world," and the terms "world" and "worldly" are used here in the sense in which they are presented in the scriptures, e.g., "the wicked," or those who oppose the righteous or who adopted a wicked lifestyle. Such individuals are "of the world," while the Lord and His followers are not (see John 17:14–16; James 4:4; D&C 53:2).

6. Dallin H. Oaks, *Ensign*, November 1986, 20.

7. John Leo, "Thou Shalt Not Command," *U.S. News and World Report*, 18 November 1996, 16.

8. Ibid. John Leo also mentions, "some insist that any new set of commandments be called the Ten Tentative Suggestions." And later, "[a]nother way out of the commandment dilemma is to keep the bossy language of the original 10, but add some modern loopholes and explanatory matter."

9. David O. Mckay, *Gospel Ideals* (Salt Lake City: *Improvement Era*, 1953), 498.

10. James E. Faust, *Ensign*, November 1986, 10.

11. *History of the Church*, 6:198.

12. *TPJS*, 22.

13. *TPJS*, 347.

14. *History of the Church*, 1:146.

15. Lyndon W. Cook, *Joseph Smith and the Law of Consecration* (Provo, Utah: Grandin Book Co., 1985), 3.

16. Ibid., 7.

17. Levi Hancock, cited in Ivan J. Barrett, *Joseph Smith and the Restoration* (Provo: BYU Religious Studies, 1965), 112.

18. Cook, op. cit., 7.

19. Orson Pratt, *Millennial Star,* 32 (11 August 1874): 498.

20. David B. Galbraith, D. Kelly Ogden, and Andrew C. Skinner, *Jerusalem: The Eternal City* (Salt Lake City: Deseret Book, 1996), 67.

21. Mark E. Petersen, *Ensign,* May 1982, 15.

22. Spencer W. Kimball, *Ensign,* November 1978, 6.

23. George Albert Smith, "Law of Honesty," *Deseret News,* January 7, 1933, Church Section, 6.

24. Mark E. Petersen, in Conference Report, October 1971, 63.

25. Harold B. Lee, *Stand Ye in Holy Places* (Salt Lake City: Deseret Book, 1974), 370.

26. Spencer W. Kimball, *The Teachings of Spencer W. Kimball,* ed. Edward L. Kimball (Salt Lake City: Bookcraft, 1982), 198.

27. Brigham Young, in *Journal of Discourses,* 14:76.

28. John Taylor, in *Journal of Discourses,*. 16:301–2.

29. O. Leslie Stone, *Ensign,* November 1975, 41.

9

"Thou Shalt Not Bear False Witness"

GUY L. DORIUS

I HAVE OBSERVED AN interesting phenomenon among active Latter-day Saints as they annually have the opportunity to evaluate their personal worthiness to enter the temple. As their bishop asks them the standard recommend questions about tithing, chastity, the Word of Wisdom, and other issues of faithfulness, their responses are generally precise and simple. With a "yes" or a "no" they declare their eligibility to go to the temple. But for some there appears to be a different struggle when asked the question, "Are you honest in your dealings with your fellowmen?" This question often solicits the response, "I try to be," or "I think I am." At this point I'll often return to the question about chastity and have them respond with the same hesitancy.

Guy L. Dorius is a member of the Religious Education faculty at Brigham Young University, where he teaches Doctrine and Covenants and LDS Marriage and Family. He and his wife, Vicki, are the parents of four children.

This never makes them terribly comfortable, and it invites us to visit about personal integrity.

What is it about honesty that makes this question seem so difficult? Perhaps an examination of its foundations in biblical law and its application today will help in understanding our struggle with the vital issue of honesty. This investigation will also necessitate a brief analysis of the cultural climate in order to understand our need to return to a standard of honesty which is at odds with the world's expectation. The words of modern prophets will help in our desire to step beyond the culturally deprived levels of honesty and rise to God's requirement of integrity.

THE LAW

As Moses brought the stone tablets down from Sinai he delivered a law prepared for a fallen people. In the law it states, "Thou shalt not bear false witness against thy neighbour" (Exodus 20:16). The Lord reiterated this commandment both to the Nephites in Book of Mormon times and to the people He taught during His earthly ministry. It seems that later, during the Restoration, He divided this commandment into at least two different ideas. First He stated: "Thou shalt not lie; he that lieth and will not repent shall be cast out" (D&C 42:21). Later in the same section He said: "Thou shalt not speak evil of thy neighbor, nor do him any harm" (D&C 42:27).

Are there differences between the law given to the children of Israel in Moses' day and the law of the gospel given to the Church during the Restoration? In the Joseph Smith translation of the Bible there is evidence that there were changes in the law according to the righteousness of the people. It states:

And the Lord said unto Moses, Hew thee two other tables of stone, like unto the first, and I will write upon them also, the words of the law, according as they were written at the first on the tables which thou brakest; but it shall not be according to the first, for I will take away the priesthood out of their midst;

therefore my holy order, and the ordinances thereof, shall not go before them; for my presence shall not go up in their midst, lest I destroy them.

But I will give unto them the law as at the first, but it shall be after the law of the carnal commandment; for I have sworn in my wrath, that they shall not enter into my presence, into my rest, in the days of their pilgrimage. Therefore do as I have commanded thee, and be ready in the morning, and come up in the morning unto mount Sinai, and present thyself there to me, in the top of the mount. (JST, Exodus 34:1–2)

This passage reminds us that the law presented to Moses and the children of Israel was "as at the first," yet adjusted to their level of righteousness. It was intended to help them out of their carnal existence. An examination of the Old Testament and some examples of this law will help in determining its application in today's world.

THE OLD TESTAMENT

It appears that in the Old Testament certain notable individuals violated the commandment not to bear false witness. An example is found in Rahab, who lied to protect the Israelite spies from death (see Joshua 2). Later, in Hebrews 11:31, Rahab is used as an example of great faith.

Abraham may stand out even more than Rahab as an exception (see Genesis 12:10–26). We often try to dismiss Abram's (Abraham) telling the Egyptians that Sarai was his sister as being by way of custom or culture. He may very well have lied to protect himself from death and her from rape.

With these two examples it appears that there were occasions where it was appropriate to "bear false witness" when there was appropriate cause. The problem then arises as to when we might have good cause to bear false witness.

Perhaps one answer might be found in the historical context. In referring to the case of Rahab, Rushdoony writes: "To return to the matter of truth-telling, the Christian is under obligation to God to tell the truth at all times where normal communication exists. This truth-telling means, not the exposure of our privacy, but bearing a true witness in relation to our neighbor. It does not apply to acts of war. Spying is legitimate, as are deceptive tactics in warfare. Protection from thieves requires concealment and walls."[1]

In these two Old Testament examples there appears to be a choice between protection of life and truth-telling. A choice is made for the higher good. The children of Israel always had the obligation to tell the truth except in cases that would give advantage to the enemy or allow for rape, murder, or other war-like acts.[2] The Prophet Joseph Smith taught this same principle. In addressing the issue of sharing truth with the enemies of the Church he stated: "All we have said about them is truth, but it is not always wise to relate all the truth. Even Jesus, the Son of God, had to refrain from doing so, and had to restrain His feelings many times for the safety of Himself and His followers, and had to conceal the righteous purposes of His heart in relation to many things pertaining to His Father's kingdom."[3]

It must also be noted here that in the Pearl of Great Price account of Abraham there is additional information helpful in understanding when it might have been appropriate to bear false witness. The scripture reads:

> And it came to pass when I was come near to enter into Egypt, the Lord said unto me: Behold, Sarai, thy wife, is a very fair woman to look upon;
> Therefore it shall come to pass, when the Egyptians shall see her, they will say—She is his wife; and they will kill you, but they will save her alive; therefore see that ye do on this wise:
> Let her say unto the Egyptians, she is thy sister, and thy soul shall live.
> And it came to pass that I, Abraham, told Sarai, my wife, all that the Lord had said unto me—Therefore say unto them, I pray thee, thou art my sister, that it may be well with me for

thy sake, and my soul shall live because of thee. (Abraham 2:22–25.)

This differs from the biblical account in clarifying that the Lord is the one who commands Abraham to have his wife state that she is his sister. This detail is missing in the Genesis account. This important addition helps clarify when it might be appropriate to tell a lie. As in the Book of Mormon account of Nephi slaying Laban, the only one who could override the law was the lawgiver. The Lord had to command Nephi to kill Laban, contrary to the law Nephi understood, just as He had to command Abraham to have Sarai lie.

A word of caution is appropriate at this point. The previous discussion is not intended to give licence to lying. Even in the Old Testament the Lord shows He felt strongly about false witnesses. Proverbs states:

These six things doth the Lord hate: yea, seven are an abomination unto him:

A proud look, a lying tongue, and hands that shed innocent blood,

An heart that deviseth wicked imaginations, feet that be swift in running to mischief,

A false witness that speaketh lies, and he that soweth discord among brethren. (Proverbs 6:16–19.)

This lists both lying and bearing false witness as things the Lord hates. And when He came to fulfill the law, He did not dismiss us from our obligation to be truthful. If there was to be any change in the law, it would likely be to persuade us to live it more fully.

TODAY

This brings us to a discussion of our days. With the overriding principle of honesty still in force, why is it so difficult to answer the question; "Are you honest in your dealings with your fellowmen?" I doubt that when we struggle with this issue it is because we have had to lie in order to preserve life or virtue. We likely have not been at war or felt it necessary to hide spies. Many of the Old Testament justifications don't seem to fit. I especially do not perceive that many of us have been commanded of the Lord to bear a false witness. Perhaps part of the reason we struggle with honesty can be found in the cultural environment we live in.

In the United States there has been a constant erosion of values over the years that has shaken the very foundations of our morality. Along with every other value, honesty has taken a beating. Stephen L. Carter made an observation while watching a football game with his children. He describes that during the game a player who was supposed to have made a catch did not. He acted like he did, and the referee missed the call and signaled it complete. This was before the instant replay rule, and the call stood. Carter said that the whole viewing audience was aware that the catch had not been made. He speculates as to what the outcome would have been if the player had told the referee the truth:

> Now, suppose that the player had instead gone to the referee and said, "I'm sorry, sir, but I did not make the catch. Your call is wrong." Probably his coach and teammates and most of his team's fans would have been furious: he would not have been a good team player. The good team player lies to the referee, and does so in a manner that is at once blatant (because millions of viewers see it) and virtually impossible for the referee to detect. Having pulled off this trickery, the player is congratulated: he is told that he has made a heads-up play. Thus, the ethic of the game turns out to be an ethic that rewards cheating.[4]

This is a scenario that most of us can relate to. We have all witnessed something similar to this and brushed it off as part of the game. Perhaps we should consider what it means about our cultural integrity. Football could not be considered a time of war. Lives are not hanging in the balance. Perhaps we feel that there is one ethic for game playing and another one for living.

I was alarmed at the response I would receive when as a high school teacher I would ask a class of Latter-day Saints if they had ever cheated on a test. In these informal anonymous surveys over 90 percent indicated they had cheated. Though not terribly scientific, the results were depressing. As the students would discuss their reasoning, it became apparent that winning, or in this case getting the good grade, was much more important than honesty. I suspect what fosters this kind of thinking in our culture is the erosion of absolute truth. As a society, we have dismissed God from our very existence. We can't pray to Him in public or acknowledge His influence. Believing in Him represents "a kind of mystical irrationality."[5]

Because of our dismissal of the law-giver, His laws become abstract. Without a solid basis for truth, we are left with relativism. We then begin to make our choices depending on the situation rather than basing our decisions on truth. A rational choice becomes the preferred choice. Professor Carter has suggested, "The consistent message of modern American society is that whenever the demands of one's religion conflict with what one has to do to get ahead, one is expected to ignore the religious demands and act . . . well . . . *rationally*."[6]

This rational approach leaves us with the opportunity to choose when we think it would be appropriate to lie and when it is not. Unlike the Old Testament examples previously cited, there is no standard of war or morality here; and without God as the guide we can hardly claim divine revelation as our justification for a lie. We are therefore left with real questions about the validity of our dishonesty. Society being without an anchor, lying has become rampant. In 1971 Elder Mark E. Petersen asked: "But in our society is there anything more widespread than the tendency to lie and deceive?"[7]

Elder Petersen then proceeded to list a litany of ways in which our culture answers affirmatively to his question. It is obvious he was convinced that dishonesty is one of our major concerns in today's society.

It is fortunate that, as Latter-day Saints, we know there is a God and that His prophets and scriptures are among us. When the law is attached once again to the law-giver, we regain our moral compass. We realize that if we were to ever legitimately need to lie, the Lord would let us know. But through His prophets we are given counsel which aids us in our attempt to escape the deceit of our day. As previously mentioned, the law in the Doctrine and Covenants suggests two dimensions of this commandment for us today: "Thou shalt not lie" and "Thou shalt not speak evil of thy neighbor, nor do him any harm." (D&C 42:21, 27.) The scriptures and the words of the prophets invite us to understand that these are closely related. A discussion of lies will lead to an understanding of the harm we might do to our neighbor.

As Elder Petersen pointed out, lies can take various forms. We might lie to cover a sin. We might lie to protect our image or even to take advantage. We can lie to others, to ourselves, and we can attempt to lie to God. But after all is said and done, a lie is a lie. The scriptures make reference to those who lie and believe they are justified. In one instance Joseph Smith had lost the first manuscript of the Book of Mormon through Martin Harris. The Lord revealed to Joseph the plan of his enemies to change the manuscript in order to catch him in what they supposed was a lie. The scriptures read:

> Yea, he saith unto them: Deceive and lie in wait to catch, that ye may destroy; behold, this is no harm. And thus he flattereth them, and telleth them that it is no sin to lie that they may catch a man in a lie, that they may destroy him.
>
> And thus he flattereth them, and leadeth them along until he draggeth their souls down to hell; and thus he causeth them to catch themselves in their own snare. And thus he goeth up and down, to and fro in the earth, seeking to destroy the souls of men. Verily, verily, I say unto you, wo be unto him that lieth to deceive because he supposeth that another lieth to deceive, for such are not exempt from the justice of God. (D&C 10:25–28.)

The Lord indicates that one of the ways Satan persuades us to be dishonest is by making us believe it is appropriate to lie in order to catch another in a lie. The outcome of such logic is evident in the scripture. It is evident that lying is one of those things the Lord hates (see Proverbs 6:16–17).

Sometimes we try to evaluate whether a lie is big or small. I have yet to see a distinction scripturally. The trap is often set for us to believe in the "white lie." This is reminiscent of Nephi's warning of our day, wherein he stated: "And there shall also be many which shall say: Eat, drink, and be merry; nevertheless, fear God—he will justify in committing a little sin; yea, *lie a little* (2 Nephi 28:8, emphasis added)."

And more recently Elder Marvin J. Ashton taught: "In recent days all of us have witnessed many who have weakened themselves even to the point of falling completely as they have sacrificed the leading principles of honesty and integrity in order to climb an artificial ladder of accomplishment. No lasting great personal heights are ever reached by those who step on others to try to push themselves upward. It is not surprising to learn that people who tell white lies soon become color-blind."[8]

Elder Ashton's classic statement about white lies suggests that we cannot afford to try to distinguish between colors of lies. We would do well to avoid all lies.

There are even more subtle ways for us to be trapped in a lie. President Spencer W. Kimball suggested that another way of bearing false witness is to "debate" or argue knowing full well that you are on the wrong side of an issue. He taught that this often occurs in politics or religion. He suggested that it occurs in our Sunday School classes. He stated: "In the Church we have teachers who develop in a class an argument which they call discussion and, on pretense of getting participation, damage the faith of class members. I heard of one teacher who proposed to his class during a lesson on the divinity of Christ's mission that he, the teacher, would take the position that Christ was an impostor and his work a fake. The class was to defend Christ's divinity. Being so well prepared and with his class taken unawares, the teacher proved by logic that Christ was a fraud—or at least, when the class was dismissed some vital questions were unanswered and the issue was still undetermined. The man loved to debate, to argue. But his witness was false."9

It is apparent that we are under an obligation to bear a true witness in all circumstances, especially when we are bearing witness of the gospel. As the gospel of Jesus Christ is established by the law of witnesses, our witness of it must be true and the doctrine we testify of must be pure. Elder Bruce R. McConkie suggested:

> To testify falsely about the truths of salvation, or to claim truth and verity for a false system of salvation, is also to bear false witness. According to the Lord's system, almost all things are established in the mouths of witnesses. Apostles and seventies, for instance, are given the special calling of standing as especial witnesses of the name of Christ. Every member of the Church is obligated to be a witness of the restoration. Those, however, who teach false doctrines are bearing false witness; and those who claim, falsely, that salvation is found in some system other than the very one ordained by Deity are bearing record of that which is not true — and along with all false witnesses will be rewarded according to their deeds.10

That our testimonies must be true or we risk bearing false witness puts a heavy burden on us as believers. We must be found standing for the gospel at all times.

The Lord also reminds us of our obligation not only to speak truth but to act truthfully. As well as being warned about speaking evil of our neighbor, we are reminded that we should not "do him any harm" (D&C 42:27). The teachings of the Brethren are replete with reminders of our obligation not to gossip and malign our fellowmen. President Kimball reminded us of the far-lasting effects of gossip when he stated: "Lies and gossip which harm reputations are scattered about by the four winds like the seeds of a ripe dandelion held aloft by a child. Neither the seeds nor the gossip can ever be gathered in. The degree and extent of the harm done by the gossip is inestimable."[11]

We cannot afford to be spreading rumors and lies about our neighbors. Even though we may feel that we have accurate information, we must consider the damage done by thoughtless words. Remember the Lord's admonition to "strengthen your brethren in all your conversation, in all your prayers, in all your exhortations, and in all your doings" (D&C 108:7).

Another aspect of our struggle with honesty is found in our business dealings. Too often we don't consider the harm we do to others in a shady business deal. Elder Dallin H. Oaks taught us our responsibility by suggesting:

> Scheming promoters with glib tongues and ingratiating manners deceive their neighbors into investments the promoters know to be more speculative than they dare reveal.
>
> Difficulties of proof make fraud a hard crime to enforce. But the inadequacies of the laws of man provide no license for transgression under the laws of God. Though their method of thievery may be immune from correction in this life, sophisticated thieves in white shirts and ties will ultimately be seen and punished for what they are. He who presides over that Eternal Tribunal knows our secret acts, and he is "a discerner of the thoughts and intents of the heart" (Hebrews 4:12; D&C 33:1).[12]

The business world may be the real testing ground of our integrity. So much is rationalized away as just doing business. How careful we must be to not misrepresent a situation or hide some vital information! God will bless us in our desire to deal honestly one with another.

CONCLUSION

This chapter has covered both the historical and present-day applications of the ninth commandment. There may have been instances allowed by the Lord where an untruth was told. These were and are the exception. We live under the law today and have an important obligation to bear a true witness in all things and at all times. We would do well to remember the admonition of President Kimball: "Not only should we never bear false witness against neighbors, but the scriptures tell us we should love our fellowmen, serve them, speak well of them, build them up."[13]

Our personal integrity is on the line each day as we live with and serve our neighbors. By preserving it, we are blessed and we will bless the lives of others.

Notes

1. Rousas John Rushdoony, *The Institutes of Biblical Law* (n.c.: The Craig Press, 1973), 544.

2. Rushdoony, *Institutes*, 548.

3. Joseph Smith, *Teachings of the Prophet Joseph Smith*, sel. Joseph Fielding Smith (Salt Lake City: Deseret Book, 1976), 392.

4. Stephen L. Carter, *Integrity* (New York: Harper Perennial, 1996), 5.

5. Stephen L. Carter, *The Culture of Disbelief* (New York: Basic Books, 1993), 7.

6. Carter, *The Culture of Disbelief*, 13.

7. Mark E. Petersen, "Honesty, a Principle of Salvation," *Ensign*, December 1971, 72.

8. Marvin J. Ashton, "Strengthen the Feeble Knees," *Ensign*, November 1991, 71–72.

9. Spencer W. Kimball, *The Miracle of Forgiveness* (Salt Lake City: Bookcraft, 1969), 53.

10. Bruce R. McConkie, *Mormon Doctrine*, 2d ed. (Salt Lake City: Bookcraft, 1966), 75.

11. Kimball, *Miracle*, 54.

12. Dallin H. Oaks, "Brother's Keeper," *Ensign*, November 1986, 20.

13. Kimball, *Miracle*, 99.

10

"Thou Shalt Not Covet"

JAMES A. CARVER

AVING READ THE FIRST nine commandments, a person might wonder why God included the tenth commandment, "Thou shalt not covet," when it is already embodied in the seventh and eighth commandments. It seems to be a repetition, a continuation, or an extension of the seventh commandment, "Thou shalt not commit adultery," and the eighth commandment, "Thou shalt not steal." The tenth commandment is different, however, to the extent that it begins its focus first in the heart, before it erupts into the full deed. This commandment centers on the internal flaw of evil desires and thoughts, while the seventh and eighth commandments focus on the external acts of the heart.

James A. Carver is associate director of the Cedar City Institute of Religion, adjacent to the campus of Southern Utah University. He has taught in the Church Educational System for thirty-four years. He and his wife, Merilyn, are the parents of ten children.

In its fullest extension, the tenth commandment evidently is the basis for someone breaking any or all of the previous nine commandments. Elder Richard L. Evans wrote: "The tenth commandment is inseparably integrated with all the others, and coveting could lead to infraction of all the others—for there is a wholeness in life in which each part complements the other." [1]

The tenth commandment is a very appropriate last commandment. When we overcome covetousness we are less likely to break any of the other nine commandments.

THE TEXT

Thou shalt not covet thy neighbour's house, thou shalt not covet thy neighbour's wife, nor his manservant, nor his maidservant, nor his ox, nor his ass, nor any thing that is thy neighbour's (Exodus 20:17).

Neither shalt thou desire thy neighbour's wife, neither shalt thou covet thy neighbour's house, his field, or his manservant, or his maidservant, his ox, or his ass, or any thing that is thy neighbour's (Deuteronomy 5:21).

The word *covet,* or a form of the word, occurs forty-one times in the Bible but only three times in the Book of Mormon and eight times in the Doctrine and Covenants. It is important that we understand the meaning of the two Hebrew words that are translated "covet" and "desire" as they are used in this great epitomic commandment.

In Exodus 20:17, the word translated "covet" is the Hebrew word *chamad,* which means "to desire, to covet, to delight in or be pleased by."[2] Deuteronomy 5:21 uses two words, *desire* and *covet,* which in Hebrew are *taavah* and *chamad. Taavah* means "to lust, or desire."[3] *Chamad* is the same Hebrew word as found in the Exodus account. The Greek Old Testament, called the Septuagint,[4] renders the Greek word *epithumaseis* in both places in the Deuteronomy account and in the singular usage in Exodus. It means "to set one's heart upon, lust after, long for, covet, or desire."[5]

Some may consider the use of the term *neighbor,* in the tenth commandment, to be restrictive,[6] but the Savior made it clear who our neighbor is when He was quizzed about this by a lawyer (see Luke 10:25–37). Jesus' explanation was that anyone who is in need of our assistance is our neighbor.[7] Neither is it meant to be a limiting term in the Decalogue.[8] There too it means anyone we know who needs help that we gan give; or, in the negative sense, who has something we might covet. Thus anyone, or everyone, could potentially be our neighbor.

Furthermore, because of its nature, breaking the tenth commandment could cause one to break any or all of the other nine commandments.

COVETOUSNESS AND LUST

Covetousness is a close companion of lust. As mentioned above, the Hebrew word for *covet* includes also the meaning, "to lust." Lust is greedy, self-serving, and evil. Its opposite, love, is giving, caring, and nurturing. It is a wise God who in the first commandment teaches us to love God and in the last commandment warns us of abusing that love through lust and covetousness.

Godlike love, or *agape,* as used in the New Testament, is the extension of oneself to another. It means to give that which is good, or needed; to nurture, sacrifice, be kind, and enrich. To lust, or covet, is to seek to take from, to extort, to indulge in or seek self-gratification at the expense of others. It is destructive because it takes away and robs from another. It even kills and destroys. Love builds, restores, lifts and makes whole. Love is selfless, while lust is selfish. To covet is to prepare to commit a multitude of sins.

In the premortal world, Satan coveted the position held by Jesus. Satan wanted Jesus' power, honor, and glory, but he did not want or seek the ultimate welfare of others. Although Satan wanted Jesus' position, he never would have given his life for us. He had no intention of sacrificing himself so that we could be exalted sons and daughters of God. He sought to take away man's agency in order to control and manipulate mankind according to his lusts for power and glory.

King David coveted the wife of Uriah the Hittite. His covetousness of Bathsheba led him to take Uriah's wife in adultery and then to murder the faithful Uriah. David's story is one of the saddest in scripture. Nevertheless, many Davids have fallen because they coveted that which was forbidden. President Kimball taught us in his pamphlet, *Love vs. Lust,* that lust is not a form of love but is its antithesis. If David had loved Bathsheba—he hardly knew her—he would not have taken her from her husband, who in many ways was a greater man than King David. In the process of David's lust for Bathsheba he broke not only the tenth commandment but also the fifth, sixth, seventh, eighth, and ninth commandments. David did not honor his parents, or his other wives. He did not honor the sanctity of life, or the sanctity of marriage. He stole Uriah's wife and Bathsheba's virtue, and he lied in his dealings with Uriah, Bathsheba, and especially God.

How the great have fallen when the tenth commandment is broken! The righteous have suffered by the wicked deeds of the covetous, and the covetous by their own deeds. Joseph Smith was put to death by people who coveted his power and glory. Even some who had been close to him in his work began to covet his abilities, power, and honor; which coveting finally fulfilled itself by the prophet's untimely death by murder.

God's children need to take the tenth commandment more seriously. Its violation is an insidious cancer that can attack any or all of Sinai's commandments.

COVETOUSNESS AND PRIDE

The sin of covetousness is one of the first symptoms of pride, and pride is the sin that, according to prophecy, will be the greatest detriment to the Saints in the last days. To covet a neighbor's wife or possessions is no different from one whose pride causes him to acquire wives and wealth at the expense of others. The prophet Moroni was very concerned about the covetousness and pride that would exist in the "holy church of God" in the last days. He wrote:

Behold, I speak unto you as if ye were present, and yet ye are not. But, behold, Jesus Christ hath shown you unto me, and I know your doing.

And I know that ye do walk in the pride of your hearts; and there are none save a few only who do not lift themselves up in the pride of their hearts, unto the wearing of very fine apparel, unto envying, and strifes, and malice, and persecutions, and all manner of iniquities; and your churches, yea even every one, have become polluted because of the pride of your hearts.

For behold, ye do love [covet] money, and your substance, and your fine apparel, and the adorning of your churches, more than ye love the poor and the needy, the sick and the afflicted.

O ye pollutions, ye hypocrites, ye teachers, who sell yourselves for that which will canker, why have ye polluted the *holy church of God?* Why are ye ashamed to take upon you the name of Christ? Why do ye not think that greater is the value of an endless happiness than that misery which never dies— because of the praise of the world?

Why do ye adorn yourselves with that which hath no life, and yet suffer the hungry, and the needy, and the naked, and the sick and the afflicted to pass by you, and notice them not? (Mormon 8:35–39; emphasis added.)

It wasn't just the world that Moroni was worried about, it was also the "holy church of God." It seems that the sins of pride and coveting will threaten the Church in the last days.

Coveting is the wanting of something. Pride is the obtaining of things wanted, things that ofttimes belong to someone else, or are more needed by someone else. Coveting and pride are tandem evils that alienate one from God and from one's earthly, spiritual peers. These twin relics of materialism are the downfall of individuals, communities and countries. They produce a one-way ticket to the telestial kingdom. The problem in the world isn't the scarcity of money or production, but the distribution of wealth and produce; and that is the problem of coveting and pride. This strikes at the very heart of the rich. Granted, the poor can covet the rich and be prideful in their own way, but the rich can affect the lives of so many that they become the focal point of national well-being.

James A. Michener, in his book, "This Noble Land," discusses the problems of the distribution of wealth in the United States. He notes in 1989 the wealthiest 1 percent of the nation's households owned nearly 40 percent of our national wealth. The top 20 percent of Americans—households worth $180,000 or more—possess more than 80% of the country's wealth.[9]

Michener further relates that during the medieval period the "Church" controlled most of the land. Since the peasants were not allowed to control this land, the "Church" grew richer while the peasants grew poorer because they now had to buy back the crops they had produced.

In a similar fashion to the European church and the peasant demise, the United States is headed toward the same problem. American wealth is accumulating into fewer hands, while at the same time government policies are favoring the rich, causing the poor to be pushed even further down the economic ladder. Michener's summary warning of this problem is in harmony with that of the prophet Moroni. Michener says:

> My knowledge of history warns me that if, like the medieval church, we allow great wealth to accumulate in a few hands, and if we continue to allow the rich to become richer while greater numbers of the middle class slide into near poverty and the poor grow ever more desperate, revolution of some kind will become inevitable. In the United States it may be long deferred, for we are still a rich and powerful land that can absorb some errors, but the potential for violence cannot be ignored. I am deeply worried about our willingness to face

up to this crucial problem of how to get spending money into the hands of the lower third of the population.[10]

Both the rich and the poor may covet, but only the rich have the realistic means to solve many of the economic problems of our day. The solution to this dilemma was given by God more than three thousand years ago: Obey the Ten Commandments! The Judeo-Christian world has no excuse for this dilemma's even existing within its own realm. The problem is that we have not kept the Ten Commandments. Even the disregarding of the tenth commandment has led us to a situation where revolution remains a constant threat to world peace and harmony. How long can we ignore Mount Sinai? It is evident that time is running out. Our world is in an emergency situation. We know the collective outcome. Only individually can we make a difference now. Our salvation, temporally and spiritually, depends on how we respond to the Ten Commandments. Israel rejected Sinai in the days of Moses. Will our covetousness cause us to do so again in our day?

Thus the violation of the tenth commandment opens the floodgates, and this could cause us to drown in the suffocating waters of pride and covetousness. Moroni could not have made it any clearer. We must not allow covetousness to run its full course. If we do, we will indeed corrupt the "holy church of God." But how can we prevent this from happening? We must prevent covetousness and pride from entering our hearts. We must realize that we cannot break the tenth commandment and remain God's chosen people. Again, what must we do to prevent this?

The solution is in understanding the history of God's kingdom and the effect the world has had upon this kingdom. It begins in our own homes and neighborhoods and communities. Both Exodus and Deuteronomy include restrictions about coveting our neighbor's property, and so on. But the word *neighbor* really means one's community. Today it would include a more extensive area. It is our whole environmental area. It includes our towns and cities. Even our country. Wherever the Saints of God are located.

The tenth commandment is our safeguard. It means that we must control our thoughts and our actions. Its intent is to prohibit improper thoughts from becoming evil deeds. This inner life—what goes on in our thoughts and dreams—is what will determine our destiny. The starting block is the heart and the mind. Our thoughts are seedlings of our actions. We should desire righteousness and be content with what is rightfully ours. Covetousness opens the doors to a barrage of sins that, once embraced, are difficult to stop.

CAIN, THE FIRST MORTAL BREAKER OF THE TENTH COMMANDMENT

The tenth commandment appears to have been the first recorded commandment broken by a mortal being after the Fall. Cain, who first broke this commandment, is the paradigm of commandment breakers. By the time he had finished his devilish schemes to separate himself from the control of Adam, he had broken almost all of the Ten Commandments.

Cain broke the first commandment when he said, "Who is the Lord that I should know him?" (Moses 5:16.) He may not have broken the second commandment, but he refused to offer a proper offering to the Lord. He broke the third commandment by offering an offering to God that was contrary to the law of sacrifice, thus defying God and the future atonement of Christ. Cain dishonored his parents by slaying Abel, which brought them great heartache, thus breaking both the fifth and sixth commandments. Cain broke the ninth commandment when he succumbed to the "father of all lies" (see Moses 4:4; 5:29–30). And, of course, Cain broke the tenth commandment in the very beginning when he coveted Abel's flocks of sheep.

SIGNIFICANCE OF THE NUMBER TEN

Since "Thou shalt not covet" is the tenth commandment, it could be helpful to explore the significance of the number 10 according to Hebrew and Jewish thought. In biblical Hebrew, the letters of the alphabet are also used for the cardinal numbers. For example, the first Hebrew letter is *aleph*, which equals, numerically, 1. *Bayith* equals 2, and so forth to the last letter *tau*, which equals 22. In the Bible and in ancient Jewish tradition the numbers are significant beyond our normal use of numbers. For example, in the book of Revelation the Apostle John uses many numbers in a symbolical manner, the number 666 being the most famous. Numerous books have been written on this subject of numbers.

In the case of the tenth commandment, the Hebrew letter *yod* represents the number 10. The number 10, by Jewish thought, "expresses completion and perfection, and its sacred character may, indeed, be derived from the fact that it is the product of three and seven, both sacred numbers."[11] The Lord said, every "tenth [animal] shall be holy unto the Lord" (Leviticus 27: 32). Rabbi Ginsburg said: "The fact that the number ten is universally accepted as the basis of the number system reflects the intrinsic nature of ten as the consummate expression of plurality. Ten serves to reveal in full the hidden spectrum of plurality inherent in every point of Creation, as well as to bring plurality 'back' to a sense of initial and essential unity."[12]

The Ten Commandments are fundamental to the well-being of God's kingdom. They are the basis for all of the other of God's commandments because they are "the consummate expression of plurality." The tenth commandment, "Thou shalt not covet," is similarly significant because its violation is the basis for the violation of all the other nine commandments. It is a plurality of all the other nine.

THE EXTENDED MEANING OF THE TENTH COMMANDMENT

The tenth commandment specifically commands one only to refrain from coveting that which belongs to one's "neighbour." But by the extension of this principle one should, in addition, not covet that which one already possesses, even if it is acquired from one's own labors. Therefore, in principle, we can break the tenth commandment by coveting the temporal things we acquire in excess that could have been shared with the poor or the needy. We can covet our own wealth by building excessively expensive houses for ourselves, and by driving the most expensive automobiles. We can covet many of the things we possess and hope to possess, by legal means, without taking from someone else. Thus, by coveting our own wealth we deny the poor, the sick, the unfortunate, the weak, and the depressed, the blessings we could bestow upon them. Elder Neal A. Maxwell addressed this subject in a 1990 conference address on selfishness. He said, "Each spasm of selfishness narrows the universe that much more by shutting down our awareness of others and by making us more and more alone."[13]

In that same conference, he said:

> Stubborn selfishness leads otherwise good people to fight over herds, patches of sand and strippings of milk. All this results from what the Lord calls coveting "the drop," while neglecting "the more weighty matters."[14]

To those who covet their own possessions the Lord has said: "Let them repent of all their sins, and of all their covetous desires, before me, saith the Lord; for what is property unto me? saith the Lord. . . . Is there not room enough on the mountains of Adamondi-Ahman. and on the plains of Olaha Shinehah, or the Land where Adam dwelt, that you should covet that which is but the drop, and neglect the more weighty matters?" (D&C 117:4, 8.)

The poor may covet the wealth of the rich, but the rich often covet the same wealth they already own. They want it for themselves. Again, it isn't that there is insufficient wealth in the world or the land; but that there is an insufficient distribution of that wealth, land, and produce. Thus we are not only guilty of coveting our neighbor's possessions; we as a people are often guilty of coveting our very own possessions. Coveting is a sin of the rich as well as the poor.

The Lord has warned the Saints: "Now, I, the Lord am not well pleased with the inhabitants of Zion, for there are idlers among them, and their children are also growing up in wickedness; they also seek not earnestly the riches of eternity, but their eyes are full of greediness" (D&C 68:31).

We may also covet the things of the world to the extent that we go deeply into debt. We covet things beyond our ability to pay, resulting in heavy debt and even bankruptcy. High interest rates and excessive borrowing become a burden we seldom escape. President J. Reuben Clark spoke of this financial thief in a general conference address in 1938. He said:

> Interest never sleeps nor sickens nor dies; it never goes to the hospital; it works on Sundays and holidays; it never takes a vacation; it never visits nor travels; it takes no pleasure; it is never laid off work nor discharged from employment; it never works on reduced hours; it never has short crops nor droughts; it never pays taxes; it buys no food; it wears no clothes; it is unhoused and without home and so has no repairs, no replacements, no shingling, plumbing, painting or white-washing; it has neither wife, children, father, mother, nor kin-folk to watch over and care for; it has no expense of living; it has neither weddings nor births nor deaths; it has no love, no sympathy, it is as hard and soulless as a granite cliff. Once in debt, interest is your companion every minute of the day and night; you cannot shun it or slip away from it; you cannot dismiss it; it yields neither to entreaties, demands, or orders; and whenever you get in its way or cross its course, or fail to meet its demands, it crushes you.[15]

In summary, those who covet have sought for happiness and success in the acquisition of wealth, power, and pleasure for their own personal gain. They neglect to comprehend that failure to include all in the advancement of self only results in a competitive race to outdo others by acquiring more than others have.

We covet in three main areas: wealth, power and pleasure; or, in other words, the carnal, sensual, and devilish. The carnal brings the pleasures of the body, the sensual maximizes the bodily thrills in sexual promiscuity and sin; and the devilish is self-seeking, power-seeking, and getting gain at the expense of others. Coveting is the ultimate of sensuality. It is the black hole of human carnality. It can only make gains at the expense or deprivation of someone else.

Unless the poor refuse to work, the poor needn't be poor if the rich would share. There is enough money in the world for all to secure the necessities of life and become happy. But the needed distribution of wealth will never happen as long as people covet. To covet is to steal. To covet is to kill. To covet is to commit adultery or fornication. To covet is to hoard. To covet is to lie and deceive. To covet is to deprive others. Fortunately, all who covet don't overtly do all of these things. But, if they continue to covet, the seed of the outward action has been planted, and if given the opportunity it will manifest itself in the full bloom of iniquity.

To covet is a sin, a grievous sin, even though it may be the little league of major league sins. It is the incubation of greater sins. It is an engine that pulls a long train of sins and iniquities to fruition. It is the motivation behind a multitude of sins. No wonder the Lord gave it as the tenth commandment. It is the driving power of almost all other sins. Satan and Cain were its prime exemplars.

THE SOLUTION

The solution to the problem of covetousness is to learn to love and serve the Lord and His children. This kind of love is usually called *agape* in the Greek New Testament, and it is usually translated as charity, or love. It is the "pure love of Christ." Agape is not easily acquired, but it is necessary for all who will faithfully serve the Lord.

When the Savior was about to leave the Apostles and ascend back to His Father, He had some parting words of counsel with

His servant Peter. After dining with the Apostles, and perhaps others, Jesus had a private discussion with this Apostle who was soon to be given the full responsibility for the Church. This beautiful dialogue between Jesus and Simon Peter, though brief, is one of the most insightful accounts of the Savior's teachings. Astounding in its simplicity, yet marvelous in its power. The account is found in John 21:15–18. The Greek words are taken from Nestle's Greek Text.

> So when they had dined, Jesus saith to Simon Peter, Simon, son of Jonas, lovest [agapas] thou me more than these? He saith unto him, Yea, Lord; thou knowest that I love [philo] thee. He saith unto him, Feed my lambs.
>
> He saith to him again the second time, Simon, son of Jonas, lovest [agapas] thou me? He saith unto him, Yea Lord; thou knowest that I love [philo] thee. He saith unto him, Feed my sheep.
>
> He saith unto him the third time, Simon, son of Jonas, lovest [phileis] thou me? Peter was grieved because he said unto him the third time, Lovest [phileis] thou me? And he said unto him, Lord thou knowest all things; thou knowest that I love [philo] thee. Jesus saith unto him, Feed my sheep.
>
> Verily, verily, I say unto thee, When thou wast young, thou girdest thyself, and walkedst whither thou wouldest: but when thou shalt be old, thou shalt stretch forth thy hands, and another shall gird thee, and carry thee whither thou wouldest not.
>
> This spake he, signifying by what death he should glorify God. And when he had spoken this, he saith unto him, Follow me.

The full meaning of this great interview and dialogue with Peter cannot be fully appreciated without a little understanding of Greek. Most translations have failed to reflect the change the Savior made in the use of the word translated "lovest." There are two Greek words used here for love. One is *agape*. The other is *philos. Agape* is defined as God's love, or the highest love. It is not common among humans but can be obtainable by them. In the New Testament it is often translated as *charity*. According to Bauer's Lexicon, *agape* is the love of "super natural beings," it is "God's love for mankind." It is "the love Jesus had."[16]

Most translations miss the point in this passage. When Jesus asks Peter, "lovest thou me?" Peter does not reply with the same word for love. Peter uses *philos*, which means, "loving, kindly devoted, friend."[17] Peter is reflecting back man's love. That is why Peter was "grieved" because the third time the Savior changed His question from *agape* to *philos*. Peter is responding by saying he doesn't have *agape*. Peter was grieved because the Savior came down to Peter's level, and it was not Peter going up to the Savior's level of love. But Jesus, in a unique way, told Peter that one day he would have that higher love. While Peter is young he will go his way, but as Peter matures in faith and love he will go where the Lord wants him to go. Even if it means to be crucified as his master would be.

When this passage is read in the Greek, the dialogue between the Master and His servant is not only informative but also is special in the kind and nurturing manner in which Jesus taught His disciple a higher love.

Modern Apostles and prophets have sought this higher love, as will all Saints as they progress in the faith. Indeed, our future depends on our being filled with this love, "which [the Father] hath bestowed upon all who are true followers of his Son, Jesus Christ" (Moroni 7:48).

Covetousness is not overcome in a moment. But when one nurtures love and not pride, the victory will always be on the side of love. Charity, or the "pure love of Christ," can indeed "cover the multitude of sins" (1 Peter 4:8). It does so because "love never faileth" (1 Corinthians 13:8).

Notes

1. Richard L. Evans, *The Ten Commandments Today, A Discussion of the Decalog, Special MIA Edition* (Salt Lake City: Deseret Book, 1959), 142.

2. Gesenius, *Hebrew-Chaldee Lexicon To The Old Testament Scriptures,* (Grand Rapids: Baker Book House, 1979), 772.

3. op. cit.

4. The Greek Septuagint is the oldest complete manuscript of the Old Testament. The King James Version of the Old Testament comes from the Hebrew Massoretic text.

5. Liddell and Scott, *Greek-English Lexicon* (London: Oxford University Press, 1964), 292.

6. Meaning that only those who are closely associated with us in companionship and geography are our neighbors.

7. The Hebrew word translated *neighbor* is *raych,* meaning companion or friend.

8. *Decalogue* is another term for the Ten Commandments.

9. James A. Michener, *This Noble Land* (New York: Random House, 1996), 30.

10. Ibid., 43–44. See also Mosiah 4:16–18, where King Benjamin gives us the answer to Michener's dilemma.

11. Ronald H. Isaacs, *The Jewish Book of Numbers* (Northvale, New Jersey: Jason Aronson, Inc., 1996), 77.

12. Rabbi Yitzchak Ginsburgh, *The Aleph-Beit* (Northvale, New Jersey: Jason Aronson, Inc., 1995), 163.

13. Neal A. Maxwell, in Conference Report, October 1990, 17.

14. Ibid., 16.

15. J. Reuben Clark, Jr., in Conference Report, April 1938, 103.

16. Walter Bauer, *A Greek-English Lexicon of the New Testament and Other Early Christian Literature,* adopted and translated by William F. Arndt and F. Wilbur Gingrich (Chicago: University of Chicago Press, 1979), 4–5.

17. op. cit.

Index